# Marked in Stone

## START BUILDING YOUR
## FAMILY LEGACY

Bruce Williamson

Marked in Stone

ISBN: 978-0-9909337-0-0

# Foreword

This book came from the ashes of tragedy.

I stumbled out of my car and collapsed on the ground. My face lay on the cold concrete floor of my garage. I felt my body leaving me . . . emotionless, speechless, weightless, lifeless. I sobbed and curled into a ball. "He's gone," I whimpered. "He's gone." When my twin brother took his life without reason, without warning, without a goodbye, he didn't just break hearts but he took something from my family – his indelible mark on our unfinished story stones. I wanted my kids to know their Uncle Brian so I started writing letters to them, a journal of a desperate man finding hope in a senseless act. I started writing his legacy which became entangled in my legacy. Of Twinkies in his ear to impress girls. Of our camping nights telling stories around a fire. Of playing marine biologist and civil engineer among tide pools along the coast of Maine. Of sticking up for me when someone pushed me off the playground equipment. Of sharing a love of photographing our national parks. Of encouraging me to start-up my dog treat company with recipe ideas from his gourmet pantry. He was my best friend, my confidant, my mentor, my little brother, my big brother, a master builder, and an apprentice. I walked the days in a stinging hurt for closure that will never come, in a quiet desperation for answers that will never surface. I longed to fill the hole he left in my world now permanently changed.

But . . . then. Just a few weeks after my brother's death I received calls from the parents of two middle school boys in my church youth group. They started hinting about committing suicide on social media and wanted me to consider addressing it at the coming weekend retreat. I gathered my small group of adolescent boys together that I had been apprenticing for two and a half years and looked at them straight in the eye and painfully read them a legacy letter about my brother. Then I explained what I would have missed if I gave up at their age when I was feeling awkward, feeling alone, feeling helpless; when I didn't think I was . . . enough. I would have missed marrying the woman of my dreams when I didn't think I was handsome enough. I would have missed graduating from college and pursuing a lifelong passion in innovation with patents and new product launches and start-up enterprises when I thought I wasn't smart enough. I would have missed hugs from wonderful kids who called me "dad" when I thought I was a poor role model. I poured through a box of photos and trophies, inventions and awards, game balls and accolades from a life of giving to others when I thought I had nothing to give. I unfolded the great adventure of life - full of surprises and plot twists from a loving Father when I thought about giving up, giving in . . . when I thought that my meager starting point determined the finish line. I yelled. I cried. I hugged them. I re-labeled them and their future.

Even in your death, you gave to me so I could give to others. When you didn't think you had a song to sing, I'll sing it for you. When you didn't think you had a story to tell, you did . . . I'll tell it for you. I love you, Boo.

# Preface

Accompany reading this book with a new journal/notebook – this is your Legacy Letters journal. As you read, you will find yourself pausing at questions and provocations in contemplation. Give yourself the margin to reflect, to reminisce, to compose. Camp out on a topic or a sentence without hurry or hesitation. Set the appropriate pace on your journey toward discovery. Write fluidly. Write without filtering your words or feelings. Capture your authenticity without trying to be too smart, too funny, too correct, too polished. It will be raw and a little messy. But your words will eventually do what you want them to do. Your words will be chiseled and hewn into choice stones for building your family legacy. What you see as disjointed ramblings will be revealed as connections and patterns forming a beautiful patchwork of stories to your family. Invite and join other family members as you begin the great unfinished work of multigenerational legacy building.

# Gratitude

This book isn't mine; it's ours. To my family who reminds me every day that I'm so blessed and so wonderfully loved. To North Point Community Church for putting a mirror to my face and providing a compass for my walk. To the great story tellers in this book whose authentic letters speak volumes about their legacy – Mark, Cece, Andrea, Donna, Stephanie, Mike, Doug, Amy, Joe, Paul, Pat, Janessa, Jim, Sam, Miriam, Sue and Rick. Thank you to Mike, Stephanie, Mark, Chris, Tim, Bill, Alex, Amy, Sue, Steve, and Andy for your belief in this project and giving me the steadfast encouragement to complete it.

# Table of Contents

CHAPTER I

# The Invitation For Legacy Creation

*"What feats of human ingenuity and perseverance enabled ordinary human beings, using rudimentary tools and technologies and working under extremely difficult circumstances, to transform blocks of stone, lengths of timber, ingots of lead, pieces of iron, mountains of sand and quicklime into majestic works of art?"* - Robert Scott, *The Gothic Enterprise*

## Some of history's finest architects, builders and planners

No matter how you look at it, cathedral building was an impressive undertaking. Across the expanse of Europe, from as far north as Scandinavia to the southern shores of the Iberian Peninsula and from the rugged coast of Wales to the bucolic river basins of Eastern Europe, there are hundreds of great cathedrals built over a period of only several hundred years. Some experts estimate that between 1050 and 1350, more stone was cut in France alone than at any period in the entire history of Egypt. These monuments of faith were built by some of the world's greatest yet nameless architects, artisans, craftsmen and laborers. They used simple materials - stone, timber, sand, and ore – coupled with surpassing ingenuity, keen resourcefulness, fortitude and unwavering conviction. Absent were equations for structural engineering, resource planning spreadsheets, formal trade schools for masonry, carpentry, or glassworks. Plentiful was an unremitting commitment to firm beliefs and a resolute duty to descendants whom they would never meet. For many cathedral building was the great unfinished work, so they steadfastly apprenticed the next generation. Precious handmade tools were passed down from fathers with gratification and splendid esteem.

Despite a remarkably limited understanding of higher order mathematics and engineering, the great cathedrals were the pinnacle of technology during their time. They were a conduit for the creative energy of medieval European society. New construction and architectural techniques, such as vaulted ceilings and flying buttresses emanated from cathedrals and allowed the buildings to soar higher. Using only a limited number of tools – pickaxe, hammer, chisel, plumb, plane, saw, brace and bit, sledge hammer, auger, mathematical dividers, a set of squares, templates, a staff, a rope marked off in halves, thirds and fifths – masons, blacksmiths, and carpenters were able to construct some of the most magnificent structures ever built and the tallest in their era using just an understanding of proportion and geometry using only a single construction material – stone. John Fitchen in <u>The Construction of Gothic Cathedrals</u> writes, "Their achievement in solving their structural problems in this material has never been surpassed, or indeed even closely approached, in any other period of the world's history, the present included. The superiority of the Gothic achievement in stone over the justly great achievements in stone of the Egyptians, the Greeks…is due to the twin aims of Gothic church architecture: maximum height and light." The tools and the operation of hewing blocks of stone and carving stone ornaments have not changed since medieval times. Even the final design provided by the master architect before approval by the bishop and chapter (group of clergymen who controlled the funding) were drawn on two slabs of plaster with only two views: a floor plan and an elevation of a wall.

Every day over two tons of stone was cut, transported on carts and boats over miles of hilltops, rivers, and grassy plains simultaneously pulled by oxen and pushed by humans. Because transporting stones was expensive in time and money, quarrymen would shape the stones at the quarry before sending them to the site. To split stones for the walls, quarrymen "read" the rock face to see the lines where it would fracture. Then they drove a series of holes (patterned precisely from a template) into the stone, which made tiny tremors propagate through the stone to break it. All the stones were then carved-to-finish on the site before they were set in place. Each stone was marked by the stone-cutter, tens of thousands of intricately carved engravings. Maker's marks became a sign of pride for stonecutters. This was his splendid handiwork and his paycheck. Each stone weighing about one hundred fifty pounds was lifted as much as dozens of stories high. From medieval manuscripts, it was discovered that clever builders used an ancient Roman war invention to inspire the creation of the stone hoisting machine called a "squirrel cage." Workers could lift six times their own weight by walking in a gigantic "gerbil cage." The mortar was delivered to the masons who laid each stone on top of each other with a trowel of mortar layer. Every several minutes a stone was hoisted, placed, and secured with a mixture of sand, lime, and water in exact proportions. Any deviations could mean collapse immediately, within days, months, years.

Because of their massive size and the fact that they often had towers, spires, and domes, cathedrals were often the major landmarks in cities and countryside. Even today, the cathedral is frequently the most imposing landmark on the horizon. Built often on hills so the church could dominate the landscape, cathedral towers rise as high as four hundred-fifty feet plus the floor-to-ceiling expanse of walls and columns (called piers) of another one hundred-fifty feet for a total of nearly sixty stories! The great size and splendor of the cathedral was typically out of proportion to the town itself. The cathedral of Amiens in northern France, for example, could house the entire population of the city – some ten thousand people. Today, this is equivalent to building a stadium large enough to seat the entire city's population – perhaps, a million people. The community played the most significant role in the physical construction and day-to-day running of the cathedral. Cathedrals were not only places of worship, but also the center of daily life especially the for the lower/middle class. The cathedral was more than a place of worship; it was a marketplace, a town meeting hall, a setting for celebrations and festivals.

Cathedrals were the pinnacle of civic pride. They were a place of historic and artistic significance for a community and often played the role of telling the past through historic tombs, statues, and ornately carved furniture. Cathedrals were renowned for their decorative features such as sculptures, stained glass, frescos, arches, and vaulted ceilings. Designers used light for adornment. Walls were built containing the stone framework of the windows called tracers. Towering walls of light were a stark contrast to the darkness, dirtiness and confined conditions of daily life in medieval Europe. Light was a metaphor for God, and by designing in more light, builders hoped to bring people closer to God. Light also narrated. In an age of vast illiteracy, stained glass windows recounted stories of the Bible illuminated in vibrant color illustrations. Pulverized quartz crystal was mixed with soda ash and various metals for color then heated hotter than volcanic lava. They were poured into lead templates created by local artists to fit within the tracers. Even overcast skies tinged the walls and floors with cheerful hues. The limestone walls appeared to divinely glow even past dusk.

Cathedral building was a lifetime project across several generations. On average, the construction of the Gothic cathedrals in England took decades and even centuries from the time planning began to completion. If this effort had taken place in America, a cathedral begun at our founding in 1776 could be under construction until about 1976! Being involved in the construction of the cathedral required a willingness to be part of something larger than oneself. The people who walked through the doors of the finished cathedral were usually the great descendants of those who laid the foundation. Building started without the funds to complete it. The cost of these buildings was massive, and the money to pay for it (seen as a devotion to God) came from the community via many payments to the Church and donations from the Nobility. Despite the prejudice of the aristocracy against those who worked with their hands to earn money, cathedral building earned considerable respect because of the magnificent craftsmanship imbued in their skill. Cathedrals were entrusted to thousands who imagined, designed, and built them, but the labor pool was constantly churning and required multi-generational skill development through apprenticing. Cathedral building demanded more than skill transference to prodigy; master builders shaped the character of their apprentices ensuring they matured with perseverance, grittiness, tenacity, and attention to detail.

---

"Technology in the twelfth to sixteen centuries was rudimentary, famine and disease were rampant...yet communities with only a meager standard of living managed to make the immense investment of capital...They mobilized the spiritual and civic determination needed to sustain building projects that sometimes spanned centuries. And they created buildings whose exquisite beauty continues to amaze us."
— Robert Scott, The Gothic Enterprise

---

Above all else, cathedrals were monuments of faith. The driving force was to build a magnificent building for the glory of God, a sacred space meant to bring ordinary people closer to God. The cathedral experience was heavenly, mythical – the incredible size and scale, the Mass performed with cherubic voices, the aroma of incense, the light beaming through intricately arrayed stories from colored glass. Being involved in the construction of the cathedral required a selfless devotion to a legendary lifetime project – the squalid living, broken fingers, aching backs, frigid winters, dizzy heights.

Cathedral building was something that linked distant families together with a bond of united sacrifice, sacred hopes, shared vision. Only a few craftsmen had the satisfaction of seeing their cathedral finished in their lifetime. For the vast majority, their reward came from imagining their children and grandchildren one day praying in a building that they created; envisaging a child's bended knee in devotion; hearing the soft voices of hymns sung with reverence; the look of surprise and awe entering the cathedral for the first time. Imagine for a moment working on a project for your entire life with complete confidence that your children and grandchildren needed to finish it. Imagine the perseverance and unifying purpose. Imagine laboring every day in excessive heat, pelting rain, and damp chill with no idea how the vaulted ceiling would look completed. How would you prepare them for the great unfinished work of cathedral building?

What if we could build cathedrals in our lives? Not monuments to ourselves, but a sacred place for generations to treasure family memories, to discover life lessons, to lean on life-tested wisdom, to relish words of affirmation from mom and dad, brother and sister, to unwrap knotty life circumstances with the hindsight of trusted kin, to encounter the character of our relatives in stories from their own words, to reveal the hidden devotion of grandparents. What if we created a space where we could tell our stories in stained glass; where our light illuminated the richness, complexity, and subtleties of life for our children and grandchildren? What if we could create a place for generations to fill up their bucket when they are thirsty? What if we created a sanctuary where disoriented, discouraged family found resilience and rebound? How would we apprentice our children and grandchildren to be master builders in their families, in their communities, in their work; to mark their stones with conviction, assuredness, distinctiveness? Legacies only survive if they are passed on and picked up by the next generation.

## Legacy is for now, not for later

Legacy is present. It's living and moving. It's being shaped every day. It's not just "on" when we want it to be. It's always on - always recording, always projecting. It permeates our lives, the lives of our family members, our co-workers, our friends, our community. You are shaping the legacy of your children and grandchildren today, yesterday, tomorrow. Legacy creation is so subtle, but it is built on every word, every action, every relationship. Let it sink in – you are imprinting them – delicately, deeply.

Legacy building can be a catalyst for change to write the history we want in our families. Driven by a nagging truth that we are repeating a cycle of dysfunction. Permitting a personal hurt to haunt us. Sensing culture swaying our moral decisions, shifting our family values, controlling our financial choices. Through deep introspection, we stop wallowing in the misery of lost opportunities. We stop being dismissive about lack of time and begin creating a vision and inspiration for those behind us. We start purposefully apprenticing our family to be the men and women who can carry on the great unfinished work of building lasting legacy. What if we relentlessly pursued life now, not later? What if we mindfully authored the stories we want to tell our family?

---

"The memories we carry should be treated with respect. We should find a place to preserve them and the safest place is not in our own vessel because we will inevitably lose it or break it. We tend to be less careful with things we give ourselves, but when we receive gifts, we treat them with nurturing care. The way to preserve our memories is to give them as gifts to others." — Richard Louv, Web of Life

---

*If not you, then who?* If not you, then who will mold your boys into gentlemen? If not you, then who will tell your daughter that she is beautiful from the inside out? If not you, then who will prepare your son to be a devoted husband without wandering eyes? If not you, then who will teach your grandchildren how to live openly, loudly, without apologizes or embarrassment for their spiritual beliefs at work, in the locker room, in their classroom? If not you, then who will teach them to gratefully give more to those who have less? If not you, then who will teach them to bounce back from setbacks, to swallow their pride, to forgive, to face the truth, to hope, to stand alone, to pick up the pieces of shattered dreams and start again, to see beginnings in endings?

What if your life could be so much more to your children than foggy memories and fruitless inheritances? Can you really prepare your twenty-year-old daughter to be a great mom? Can you really implant an inner moral compass that orients your six-year-old grandson toward True North? Can you put the cancer of comparison into remission for your daughter? Can you really let your children set sail amid a culture that seems to unravel your family ties? Can you really plant the seeds of lifelong faith when they haven't seen yours? Can you really inspire your thirty-year-old son to be a great dad – selflessly beholden more to family than work? Can you undo the brainwashed images beaconing your daughter to be sexy? Can you reveal the real you – no phantom fronts or fake personas – the real you with hopes and dreams, fears and failures, cares and convictions, passions and pursuits? Can you really set an example when you haven't been? Can you teach lessons when you are still learning? Indeed. Legacy building is not waiting to answer those questions in perfect hindsight, but answering them in the future tense.

Legacy is a map and compass. Our children and grandchildren will get lost in life. Remember your first crush on a boy or girl and then finding out they didn't like you . . . am I unattractive? Remember feeling disillusioned when newlywed bliss starting wearing off and nagging emerged . . . should I leave? Remember feeling hurt when your dad stopped caring . . . should I stop loving him? Remember feeling cheated when a co-worker got credit for your work . . . should I discredit them? Remember feeling lonely from too many empty relationships that left you hurt . . . should I give in? Remember feeling shaken when your prayers for healing weren't answered . . . is faith real? What path do your children or grandchildren take in life when they get disoriented? They won't stand still. They will keep moving, but maybe in the wrong direction. Your stories can be something your family carries with them to orient their life journey. They can ask a stranger for directions or they can reach for your map and compass –"I remember that story my dad/mom told me. . . ." "Now I know what my grandmother meant when she said. . . ." Legacy stories provide them with the tools to navigate life.

---

"An individual has not started living until he can rise above the narrow confines of his individualistic concerns to the broader concerns of all humanity." — Dr. Martin Luther King

---

Legacy is a wellspring. Your family is thirsty for it. Maybe not today, but eventually. In the book, How Full is Your Bucket, the authors give us a word picture of how events, interactions, conversations, experiences, dispositions are either adding drops to your imaginary bucket or depleting your bucket. How full our bucket is affects our outlook, our mood, our self-perception, our relationships, our spirit, our feelings, our emotions. A dry bucket is thirsty – for gratitude, for positivity, for encouragement, for love, for hope. Nature abhors a void so a dry bucket will seek to be filled, maybe with the wrong people, maybe with sideways behaviors, maybe with twisted self-beliefs and destructive habits.

Studies have shown that most interactions, conversations, and events are bucket draining (30 negative to 1 positive on average every day) because we rarely apply positivity and encouragement in our everyday lives. Rarely at work, absent with classmates and school friends, far less often at home. Not only does bucket depletion cheat our families of daily joy, but it can rob them of a positive self-image. A dry bucket holder is desperate for water. Dehydrated and disoriented, they may find water in wayward circumstances or mirage relationships. Your stories can redirect negative, twisted self-perceptions inflamed by culture into a positive, healthy identity. Life circumstances and interactions can easily dry up the bucket, but only you can fill it back up. Finding giftedness in your family, experiencing joy in the everyday, unconditionally loving them, encouraging them when they need you most, listening to their dreams – bucket filling. When did you last lie in bed with your kids and tell them how much you admire them? What you see in them and why the world desperately needs them? When was the last time you told your spouse how much you cherish his/her multitude of job descriptions – Mother, Father, Chief Medical Officer, Chief Technology Officer, Headmaster, Construction Foreman, Chief Financial Officer, Executive Chef, and Head of Guest Relations? Legacy writing fills up the bucket of our family drop by drop with encouragement, approval, and hope, a spring your family returns to when life leaves them thirsty.

---

"Almost every culture of which we have detailed knowledge takes great care in managing the transition to adulthood."
— Dr. Leonard Sax, Boys Adrift

---

Legacy is a sanctuary. It's a place to rest in the love of family as you listen to affirming words from your mom and dad despite your teenage defiance. It's a place to overcome hopelessness by witnessing your family overcome adversity by leaning hard into their faith. It's a safe place of contemplation to quiet your heart from self-doubt, from your vulnerability, from weighty decisions and tough conversations. It's a place to reveal the soul of your family by listening to their quiet prayers, watching their steadfastness through the tumultuous, witnessing the subtle transformation of their heart.

Legacy is a family room with comfy couches. It's a place of laughter and inside jokes. Remember hearing the same teasing yarns about Uncle Bill or watching pranks on Aunt Emma or comic gags on grandma? It's a place of warm unity. Remember as a child listening to adults whisper half-audible stories, agape mouths, long hugs, teary eyes, sniffles, and holding hands? Your family legacy can be an encyclopedia of wisdom - true stories, real aftermaths, overflowing joy, cherished inspiration. It's a place where backstories become front stories – complacent couples learn about the real consequences of infidelity. It's a place that reveals the inner greatness of humble kin – your mom's heroic efforts raising her family without a father. It's a place where tragedy is exposed, and resilience is shouted – your mom's cancer surviving revealed her implacable inner strength. It's a place where traditions are fermented – playing football on the front lawn during halftime or cooking with your mom and grandmother in the kitchen on Thanksgiving. It's a place where your imprinting is discovered in your grandkids – your quirks, your character, your chinks, your moral fiber, your integrity, your devotion to family. It's a place with sometimes authentic and sometimes forced smiles of inner joy and choking torments. It's a room swirling with emotion, feeling, gratitude, and generational love. Most of all it's real.

Legacy is a tree. With deep, ancient roots from generations with plentiful fruit from pruning and nourishment. Branches and leaves that shade family looking for rest. Leaves that reflect the seasons of life – alive, colorful, and abundant sometimes; dormant, but not dead other times.

Legacy is choice. Every day we have choices. We can chisel, lift, and place stones to erect a cathedral, or we can let it sit for another day vacant. We can choose listening deeply to our kids or television viewing, attending recitals and games or working late, playing golf or playing catch, dinner conversations around a table or texts, gaming or taking a hike, shopping to fill an emotional void or coffee with a trusted sister. Legacy building can't wait until we aren't "so busy" . . . When will that be? Our tendency is to pass our lessons to others after our working lives settle down. Isn't that an empty promise we tell ourselves every year – "I'll spend more time . . ." or "once I retire I'm going to . . ."? How can we be sure that our family will need our wisdom at the precise moments in their life when it's perfectly convenient for us? Our influence has worth throughout different seasons of *their* life not just when we have thick margins in *our* lives. If we wait too long, we will literally miss the once-in-a-lifestage chance of influencing marriages, parenting, first jobs, first loves, first paychecks, community giving, leading people, managing money, and modeling faith.

## Getting off the treadmill

*Is this all?* Psychologists, marriage counselors, co-workers, friends – we all have heard these words in one form or another from someone usually midway through their life? We colloquially call it a mid-life crisis. A vast majority of late-career men and women, empty nesters, and retirees survey their lives and find emptiness. Many have climbed rungs in their professional ladder chasing accolades, titles, and heaping wealth. In the self-imposed race to achieve more, experience more, make more, spend more, many would paradoxically say they have less. We strive our entire lives to "be rich" with moving targets that keep changing as we achieve them. Research has found that the definition of rich is ephemeral. "Rich" when you make $35,000 a year is $70,000, but for those who made $70,000, "rich" is $150,000. When asked if those making $150,000 per year were rich – "no, those making $300,000 are." And so on through millionaires. (Even millionaires don't think they are rich – multi-millionaires are.)

---

"As mothers, we are building great cathedrals. We cannot be seen if we're doing it right. And one day, it is very possible that the world will marvel, not only at what we have built, but at the beauty that has been added to the world by sacrifices of invisible women." — Nicole Johnson, The Invisible Woman.

---

It is counter-intuitive, but happiness is not correlated with wealth. Princeton University researchers have found that link between happiness and wealth is mostly an illusion. Economist Alan Krueger and Nobel laureate Daniel Kahneman found "People with above-average income are relatively satisfied with their lives but are barely happier than others in moment-to-moment experience, tend to be more tense, and do not spend more time in particularly enjoyable activities." The Bureau of Labor Statistics survey on how people with varying income levels spend their time manifests that people with higher incomes devote relatively more of their time to work and other activities with "higher tension and stress." Refocus on a different "rich" – one that involves leaving values and cherished memories behind rather than an inheritance. Do you model to your children something more than amassing wealth as if it were a competition?

*What am I doing here?* "Here" isn't usually a physical place. Here is something different for each of us – a lifestyle, head-in-hands circumstances, work-family unbalance, a mercurial emotional state, compromised convictions, loneliness, dysfunctional habits, shattered relationships, poor financial decisions. Wealth, possessions, promotions – they can't fill the emptiness that yearns for purpose, for meaning, for renewal. We often deposit our valuable time and energy in the wrong places. Because we can measure progress at work, because we are recognized for achieving, because we can see the immediate benefits of our effort, because the reward is immediate, we tend to over-emphasize work over other life endeavors. How many moms or dads have been given a raise or a promotion or a ceremony for nailing their milestones at home? How many pats on the back do we get for our parenting "output" or family "efficiency" or "staying on budget" or "demonstrating exceptional leadership qualities"? How many of us at home get recognized for "having a great attitude"? The elusive three P's – possessions, position and power – lead to driven but disillusioned lives and eventually resentment. Culture counts score this way and in a follow-the-leader style, sons and daughters model their parents. University of Michigan professor Jeff DeGraff has been studying work-family balance issues for decades. He says, "The deeper issue is that we are addicted to work. This is not a minor issue. In our culture, work has become fundamental to our identity. It is a socially sanctioned addiction." Life has a way of slowly unraveling at first – disrespectful children, tense relationships, white lies, job stress, financial strain – then accelerates like a string on a spool running away from us. It accelerates so fast that instead of the painful process of grabbing the spool hard, we senselessly watch it unravel before our eyes. Grab your spool today. You don't need to start winding it back up, just grab it from unraveling even more.

*Dear Jonathan, Nicholas and Rachel,*

*It's eight pm . . . What am I doing here at work instead of home? I asked this question in quiet desperation in my office one night. I had a pregnant wife and a young toddler (Jonathan) at home. I was putting in more than 60-hour weeks. I was trapped in this mindset that my self-worth was a reflection of my success at work. So I buried myself in work. I prioritized it over my family. I was selfish and insecure. I'd never say it like that. When appealed by Mom, I'd say that "I am working hard to provide for my family." But it was a cover-up to a deep-seated, skewed belief that if I don't succeed at work, then I'm a failure. It was an insidious lie that I had convinced myself in high school sports, as an overachieving high school scholar, and now as a twenty-something professional. It was a message one Sunday morning that stopped me from cheating my family.*

*Culture will never tell you to work less. The cancer of comparison – how I stack up to my neighbors, my graduating class, other parents – it spreads to all facets of your life. It's insatiable. It's so easy to be pre-occupied with how we are being perceived – the neurotic anxiety of our perception. It's a deceptive treadmill - you seem to be running faster but never feel like you are getting*

*anywhere. Trust me, work moves on without you. Yes, you con-*
*tribute and they will need you, but ultimately you are replaceable*
*at work. But you are never replaceable at home. Being a devoted*
*dad and husband requires reorienting toward something more*
*lasting – building Lego cities and robots, ballroom dancing with*
*Cinderella as her prince, struggling through Algebra homework*
*together, cooking a special dinner for Mom, wrestling in the*
*basement, day hikes along rushing streams, blowing raspberries*
*on bathtub-clean bellies, praying before bed. Family-first may be*
*old fashioned but it matters. Sure you'll miss fancy dinners and*
*golf outings and 50-yard-line seats for big games. Stay home in-*
*stead. You may never be truly missed at work, but you'll always*
*be missed at home. Cheat work, not your family. You'll never*
*regret it. I never have. Love, Dad*

Maybe we need to use a different yardstick. Maybe we need to reframe our perspective – from success to significance, from acquiring
things to leaving something behind that has lasting value. It should
cause us to tremble – the awesome responsibility we have as fathers
and mothers, grandfathers and grandmothers passing on encouragement, life lessons, values to the next generation bearing our name.
Unfortunately, we have a tendency to flip-flop our priorities. We
deeply desire to make an impact in our little corner of the world, so
we journey through life desperately trying to heap wealth and prestige
and filling our hollow ego cup in the never-ending race with siblings
or neighbors. We started as purposeful parents – spending an inordi-
nate amount of time molding and shaping the moral character of our
sons and daughters, grandsons and granddaughters, nieces and nephews on the playground, in the classroom, with friends. We hover over
our children in sand pits ensuring they learn to share. We immediately
demand an apology for disrespectful words to a sibling. But then the
busyness of life seems to get in the way of purposeful teaching and
modeling. A vast majority of parents and grandparents lament over
missed opportunities usually with distant sons and daughters. When

we reverse the order of priorities, the shoddy cathedral construction from un-apprenticed children eventually spells disaster. Fractured families delicately try picking up the broken glass of isolated kids, absent parenting, splintered relationships, and missed time. If we succeed in life, but fail at home, what does that count for?

---

"There are two ways to get enough. One is to accumulate more and more. The other is to desire less." — G.K. Chesterton

---

Defining success in our life with rank, with cultish comparison, with endless appraisal is dangerous. It imprints to our family warped priorities and a never-ending strive for superlatives relative to others – grades, freestyle swim time, batting average, cars, weight, money, trophy husbands and girlfriends. What keeps your kids up at night? Their answers may surprise you. In 2013, the National Institute of Mental Health reported the prevalence of anxiety disorders among those ages 13-18 was 25.1% (30.1% for females). The incessant perfectionist mentality to "be the best" – aptly termed the "anorexia of the soul" – is leaving scores of children anxious, depressed, worn-out, passionless and with a skewed sense of self. Maybe we are asking the wrong leading questions. Not how much money will you make in that profession, but how will you make a difference in the world by pursing your passion?

*Dear Elizabeth and James,*

*Your grandparents were loving, intelligent, hardworking people without much formal education. What they lacked in education, they made up through natural curiosity and a desire for self-improvement. The values that we learned from them were "core values," those that cannot be learned and internalized in school. They are best learned at the "knee" of the ones who love and care for us. I would give my parents their Ph.D. in parenting because they really earned distinction as parents. Neither had the best experiences as children themselves because both lost fathers at an early age. Grandpa Ed's father died of illness when he was in his early teens, while Grandma Linda lost her dad to alcoholism. Therefore, neither of my parents had any roadmap to parenting. They were also very young when they married and began their own family. I was born after losing the first child at birth. My birth was followed (eighteen months later) by the birth of twins who were stricken with debilitating chronic illness. I cannot imagine being faced with this challenge at age 21 and 23. Their journey of many challenges, and the three more children that followed, did not "break" our family but only made it stronger! For me, this is the most enduring perception. How did they do it? Only an extreme amount of love, faith, and willingness to sacrifice for us helped them to continue to carry on each day. I hope you stay committed to serving those you love. I have always vowed never to do anything that would dishonor the legacy left by our parents and I hope you will too. Love, Mom*

Grandparenting is the ultimate parenting "do-over." Your sons or daughters will playback the reels of your parenting footage right before your eyes. *Was I really like that when I was stressed out? Was I that tender and gentle in my suffering? I can't believe that I would use words like that? Did they learn how to magnificently handle that circumstance from me?* You imprinted them with your parenting attitudes, beliefs, and behaviors. Your grandparenting will not erase mistakes by backtracking through time. But you can uniquely apprentice your cherished grandchildren. And in doing so you have the potential to delicately course correct your parenting. Let your children know that you made serious mistakes, have serious regrets, spring forth with joy – tell them why and then show them a better way.

We all leave something behind. Legacy is only noticeable or apparent when the builder is gone. Legacy active or passive. Legacy sweet or bitter. Remembered or forgotten. Intentional or accidental. Lasting or temporary. Funeral wisdom or jokes. Legacy building through storytelling can be the antidote for three tragedies that poison a legacy-less life.

*The Tragedy of the Unopened Gift.* We all have gifts of uniqueness. Personality traits that seem to enhance others. Matchless skills that set us apart. Passionate interests that enliven our hearts. But many are undiscovered, underutilized, unappreciated because they are buried underneath the rubble of collapsed self-impressions or submarined deep inside us because they don't align with culturally acclaimed stereotypes of success. So countless family members suppress their greatness and passion. Some aren't aware of their gifts. Some are never opened. Think of beautiful china stored away and never seen, never shared. Your storytelling can illuminate the greatness you see in them. Your storytelling can encourage family to just take a peek at their unopened gifts. Your storytelling has the potential to embolden them to follow the path of their passions, not purse. Your storytelling can show them how to balance making a living and unleashing their compassion. Your storytelling can provide the antidote for the tragedy of the unopened gift by providing the unconditional love and unconditional acceptance that your family needs to believe in themselves and be themselves.

*The Tragedy of the Ungiven Gift.* In the drone of busy lives, many of us haven't actively expressed gratefulness. Sometimes our pride or immodesty or competitiveness gets in the way of actively expressing gratitude. So countless family members whirr through life without ever knowing that they made a difference. Coaches, mentors, brothers, sisters, moms and dads, friends, grandpas and grandmas need to know that they influenced the trajectory of your choices, your paths, your life. Scientists have shown the beneficial effects of gratitude sharing on both the giver and the receiver include health, well-being, energy, empathy, optimism, happiness, resilience, and self-esteem. What's the greatest day in your grandpa's' life? Maybe when you tell him how that little dose of encouragement driving to the grocery store together when you were thirteen made an indelible mark on your life. What's the greatest day in your mom's life? Maybe when you tell her that her courageous battle through cancer unlocked hopefulness and a fighting spirit in you that you have carried into your work, your marriage, your own health crisis. Your storytelling can provide the antidote for the tragedy of the ungiven gift through the thankful gesture of writing letters to those who have influenced your life.

*The Tragedy of an Empty Life.* Scores of men and women blow past their 20s, 30s, 40s, and 50s without feeling like they achieved anything of lasting value. Legacy building isn't just for the future and it isn't wholly for others; it has a very real influence on how we live in the present. When we begin legacy building, we start living more purposefully. We are more aware that everything matters because every day you are creating legacy. We grasp that manhood and womanhood isn't something that just happens to boys and girls as they get older. They need to be apprenticed into adulthood. Your storytelling can provide the antidote for the hopelessness that your family feels in calamity – as if you wrapped your arms around him. Your storytelling can create the connection your daughter needs when she feels lonely – as if you are sitting in a chair next to her with your hands clasped in hers. Your storytelling can show your niece that your "fullness" never came from the temporary euphoria in getting but in giving.

### We all leave something behind

Every story has a beginning. Every story has an ending – every story – even yours. You do not choose the starting point, but you decide the path and the destination. Our biological family may influence our story, but it does not determine our future.

*We all leave something behind. Is it significant?* Countless souls enter their middle or golden years only to realize that they have worked for absolutely nothing of lasting value. Droves of moms and dads, retirees and middle-aged workers, grandparents and empty nesters are plagued with the question, "is this all?" A grand nobility resides in each of us – to contribute to something that outlasts our time on earth. What if we abandoned the cultural definition of success and we instead oriented toward a different goal, one that uses a different yardstick, not just standardized test scores for our kids and zeroes in our bank accounts? What if we didn't pursue success but the significance of family legacy?

*We all leave something behind. Is it lasting?* Some of us work our entire lives collecting trophies that provide no lasting satisfaction – the trophy house, the trophy car, the trophy body, the trophy job, the trophy kids, the trophy wife, the trophy stockpile. Some of us may leave behind fractured families from poor work-family balance choices; crumbling finances from debt; bloated inheritances left to unprepared descendants. Some of us may leave behind hardened hearts from ridicule; atrophied relationships from stifling rules; withdrawal from hurt and cruelty. Others invest their entire lives cherishing their spouse, children, brothers, sisters, and aging grandparents leaving behind an unshakable devotion to family. Others leave behind a generation of children whose unswerving faith is symmetrical with their behaviors. Others leave behind a spirit of citizenship – honoring and serving our country and communities. What will you imprint in the minds and hearts of your family that's multiplicative, enduring, honorable?

*We all leave something behind. Is it inspiring?* Does it arouse your progeny to carry on your great mission? Your mission may be to educate your children and encourage them to be lifelong learners. Your mission may be to teach Sunday school and spark a lifelong spiritual journey in today's youth. Will you leave behind a spirit of generosity that inspires today's youth to give more and do more for others? Will you leave behind a heart of service, protectors of the underprivileged and economically deprived? Will they pour themselves into the causes that bind us together? Will they pick up stones and finish your family cathedral in selfless devotion to the ideals you hold so deeply?

"God creates a story with each person's life – a story we were meant to tell." — Dan Allender, To Be Told

*We all leave something behind. Is it preparing?* Does it provide a life road map to desperate kin who eventually find themselves lost in the riptides of life or trapped in moral dilemmas? Are you a lighthouse for drifting relationships? Are you preparing signposts for inevitably wandering teens? Have you prepared your children for the tug-o-war between burgeoning career aspirations and anchoring family responsibilities? Have you prepared your children to sense dangerous circumstances, to see the warning signs early, to retreat, to walk away, to run fast because they are fully aware of what hangs in the balance? Are they prepared for the unfairness of debilitating health and appalling hurt and dashed dreams? What are the things that took you a lifetime to learn, but you desperately don't want them to take a lifetime to learn? Our role as parents and grandparents, aunts and uncles isn't just to feed them. Are they prepared to leave the nest? Can they fly?

Our life stories can be recognizable signposts for our children on their spiritual journey. Our stories help answer the 'how do we know when we can't see' questions of faith and the 'why do we need to' questions of obedience. We can make our spirituality real through the truth of our experiences. Not through proselytizing with rules, but with stories. They can remember the episodes, but they rarely knew what was happening inside us. Do they know why your eyes well up when you sing certain songs because they remind you of how far you've come? Do they know how you overcame your deep insecurities on your knees? Do they know how you forgave the unforgiveable even when you hurt so much? Do they know how you'd cry yourself to sleep for months? Do they know about that day you looked at yourself in the mirror and the man that you saw wasn't who you thought you'd be? Do they know that you were lost, wayward, prodigal, AWOL, but in your desperation you returned home? Do they know how good it felt

. . . like you were finally smiling again, loving again, breathing again, living for the first time?

*We all leave something behind. Are you known?* I mean really known. Not the façade, but the vulnerable you. Are there emotions that others rarely see? What are the backstories to being a great dad or a heartfelt mom? Are there things you want your family to know? Not trite sayings or prepared speeches, but the stories – amusing stories that will make their belly ache or childhood memories that will make them roll their eyes or stories that will cause them to drop tears on the page or sagas of regret and loss that will linger as they make their choices? Do they know how many times you wanted to surrender, to give in and give up, but they were your hope? Are there mistakes, errors, sins that you never want your kids to repeat or 'do-overs' you wish you had? Is the narrative your family has of you accurate? Is there something more revealing to your family than their caricature? Aren't you ready to stop pretending so they can know the real you?

Does your family know their ancestors? Not the dotted lines in genealogical diagrams, but the character-building personal histories that might otherwise soon be lost. The stories of great-grandparents who struggled as immigrants, courageously battling denigration and belittling scorn. They are the shining light, the master builders who guided us to embrace and build upon the pain, suffering, and courageous choices that formed our ethnic histories. Their stories are much needed for coming generations whose ancestral bonds have too often been detached. Like the great cathedral builders our family has stories of real heroes who sacrificed it all, committed it all, risked it all . . . in part for you.

*We all leave something behind. Is it affirming?* Do your kids know how you really feel about them . . . what you see in them, the potential, the opportunity, how you gush with pride when you tell others about them – not their goals or their grades, but their character, their maturity? Do they feel secure with themselves and your love for them? Do they feel understood and safe to talk transparently? Do they have any open wounds from unintentionality cruel things said, or are they waiting to hear you say that you are sorry? Do they know your dreams for them – not of money, but of fullness? Do they withdraw because of your perfectionist tendencies, or do they cling to you because they feel worthy of your enduring love? Everyone cherishes the approval from their mom and dad; it's something we never outgrow. Does your silence rob others of feeling noticed, prized, loved? "They just know how I feel" isn't enough. Tell them – overtly, plainly, loudly. Sometimes what we don't say speaks volumes.

What if your life had a purpose? Not just for you but for many.

What if your life was about building a cathedral? Something that spanned generations. Something that outlived you. An epic told through a collection of teachable stories to guide and guardrail decisions, to inspire and shape our children and our children's children. Is it possible to build a sacred place for your family to celebrate, to heal, and to remember? Certainly.

What if your words – not your preachy sayings or pointed finger – inspired generations of your family to live their values out loud, not in quiet seclusion? In a world seemingly herding together, mindlessly following cultural dogma, how many parents' hearts would swell seeing their children stand up, stand for, stand alone, against the grain, against the current? Is it possible to shape this fortitude in them? Positively.

What if your countless selfless acts of kindness, concealed in the busyness of life, could be seen through the eyes of a child as heroic? What if your ideals and values and life stories were procreative – what if they inspired a whole generation of family? Is it possible to inspire them to be a giver and shower the world by joyfully sharing their passions? Absolutely.

What if our sorrows and joys were there to teach us? What if our afflictions were there to hearten our children? What if we could look back on our joys and sorrows and we found abundance? What if your unfiltered, raw life story with the benefit of omniscient hindsight could help your child understand the uncinematic consequences of affairs or abuse or addiction or abandonment? Is it possible to look back on tragedy and offer a brave, durable perspective? Indeed.

What if your life was a beacon of light that showed others how to get home? We all need that beacon at some point or rather many points in our life – a tiny light in a distance on a stormy life stage that brings us home. Your story may be his light. Your story may bring her home.

What if your life was a deep embrace for someone on their knees? We all find ourselves lost in deep desperation. Your survival story may help her to get up off the floor and overcome her brokenness. Is it possible for her to fall in your arms amid the twisting storms in her life? Is it possible for your story to give her hope? Yes.

What if your life was digging wells for people to drink? When life leaves them thirsty. When the vultures circle.

What if your life – those dark, cold moments, your brokenness, your fall could bring your family closer to their faith? What if your brokenness was a catalyst for their self-change? What if they knew that your adversity was a bridge to a deeper faith relationship?

What if your goodness – your easy generosity amid less, your forgiveness amid hurt, your love amid rejection, your hope amid tragedy – alleviated the bitterness of life so they could find sweetness again?

What kind of man or woman does it take to make a permanent impact in an ailing society? In our culture it seems like everything nailed down is coming loose. Tied knots coming loose. Stalwart values chipped away. Brittle relationships nearing fracture. People are looking for the glue. Where is the glue? Can it be in the stories you tell your children?

We all leave something behind. It can be lasting or ephemeral. It can be imprinted or shallow. How will you prepare them? An inheritance is something you leave *for* them, but legacy is something you leave *in* them.

What would happen if we took ten minutes every day or a few times a week and spent time writing stories to our kids, our grandkids, our nieces and nephews? What if we all did that? What if we all brought a stone? What if you could begin building a cathedral . . . one that spanned family generations and these stories became the stones, the mortar, the stained glass, the vaulted ceilings and flying buttress columns? Just like the great cathedral builders we may never see the completion of our work, but that does not excuse us from starting the great unfinished work.

Today start building your legacy. Plank by plank. Stone by stone. With your enduring, distinctive mark on their future.

### 1.0 Quarry Questions

1. *In your Legacy Letters journal, make a list of ten things you absolutely want to leave behind to your family and then make a list of things you do not want to leave behind to your family.*

2. *What areas of your life do you seem to be pursuing success over significance?*

3. *What does "getting off the treadmill" mean for you? What gets in the way of being devoted to building your family legacy?*

### 1.0 Legacy Letters

1. *Write a letter to your family about one of the items above that you treasure and desperately want to leave behind for them.*

2. *Write about a lesson that took you a lifetime to learn, but you don't want your family to take a lifetime to uncover.*

# CHAPTER 2

# Design Principles

"So many of us in life start out building temples: temples of character, temples of justice, temples of peace. And so often we don't finish them. Because life is like Schubert's Unfinished Symphony. At so many points we start, we try, we set out to build our various temples. And I guess one of the greatest agonies in life is that we are constantly trying to finish that which is unfinishable . . . that is the story of life. And the thing that makes me happy is that I can hear a voice crying through the vista of time saying, 'It may not come today or it may not come tomorrow. But it is well that it is in thine heart.' It is well you are trying. You may not see it. The dream may not be fulfilled, but it is good that you desire to bring it into reality. It's well that it's in thine heart." — Dr. Martin Luther King

"Since my youth, O God, you have taught me, and to this day I declare your marvelous deeds. Even when I am old and gray, do not forsake me, O God till I declare your power to the next generation; your might to all who are to come." Psalm 71: 17-18 (NIV)

## Masterpieces of beauty, intrepid function

Remarkable designers do more than balance form and function; they spark emotion. Their designs enliven your senses, awaken something dormant inside you. Think about great building designs that you witnessed for the first time. What were your emotions? How did your senses react? Did you want to touch it? Did your eyes widen? Did your heart beat faster? Did you whisper when you walked inside? Did you smell something faint, but distinct? Did your gait change as you walked inside?

---

"Take a look at the craftsmanship. You see the translation of their hearts coming through their hands."
— Audre Kleven, senior project leader for the Cathedral of Our Lady of the Angels.

---

Design principles are the overarching guideposts and key tenets for sound building and visual appeal. Principles such as balance, symmetry, proportion, and contrast are often contemplated before the first stone is laid. Many cathedrals failed because either the properties of materials/engineering principles were not sufficiently understood or construction deviated from the initial plan. Historians tell us that as many as one in five cathedrals collapsed, suffered catastrophic failure, or were never completed. In Structures: Or Why Things Don't Fall Down, J.E. Gordon writes: "On the face of it, it would seem obvious that the medieval masons knew a great deal about how to build churches and cathedrals, and of course they were often highly successful and superbly good at it. Naturally, the buildings we see and admire are those which have survived: in spite of their 'mysteries' and their skill and experience, the medieval masons were by no means always successful. A fair proportion of their more ambitious efforts fell down soon after they were built, or sometimes during construction." So before we start building our family legacy, let's design it with three principles in mind:

1.  Design starts with a bold vision and a coherent plan.
2.  Without out a firm foundation, everything crumbles.
3.  Stories are the stones. Relationships are the mortar.

## 1. Design starts with a bold vision and a coherent plan

You cannot ask *what?* in the presence of great architecture, but rather *why?* Cathedrals are more than beautiful buildings. They are an expression of a community's vision and their faith. Legacy builders are dreamers. The motivation to build a monolithic cathedral springs from the heart, not the head. True, they require ingenuity, deep thinking, and extensive resource planning, but you cannot start a multi-generational project without stirring something profound inside you. Taking on the immense task of building a spiritual monument using thousands of workers over multiple generations – that idea, that dream is too big to fit neatly inside our head.

We had a vision of our family at an early age. And I can tell you with near certainty that it wasn't your daughter becoming a great surgeon, but too busy to take care of her ill sister; or your son being a workaholic and missing his kids' soccer games; or your grandson having the most expensive home in the neighborhood, but kids who go to someone else's house for dinner; or your granddaughter having more boyfriends than any other girl in high school; or your grandson being a big-headed athlete whose humility was displaced by self-importance. It was more likely that the vision we had for our family involved your daughter always coming home for Christmas; or your son being an encouraging, involved dad; or your grandson calling you up to play golf when you retired; or your granddaughter seeking your advice in marriage; or your son beseeching your counsel about tensions with a tough boss; or your daughter soliciting wisdom from you; or your son buying the more affordable home. What is your vision for your family?

Life can cast a shadow on our vision. So many of our lives don't resemble our original vision. Life takes you by surprise and suddenly your blueprint is in shambles. We tell ourselves to change our expectations, "shrink it down," "give it up," or even put it aside for 'later.' When is 'later' when every day shapes the future of your kids and grandkids? Can you afford to procrastinate when your family's future is at stake, when the ripple effects of your choices today will be encountered by generations from now? We tend to lose track of our vision from the pull of life's current – busyness, overscheduling, big projects at work, long seasons of sports, post-work exhaustion. The subtle erosion of the urgent over the important; tasks over vision. Redeem the time and pursue your vision for your family.

*Your design needs to answer "why."* Why are you building? How do you want your legacy used? Is it something that your family uses to cherish you, feel your warm presence, listen to your comforting words, smirk at your colloquialisms and mannerisms? Is it something you want your son to not just read, but remember, live by as he swims with the sharks, as he lifts toddlers on his shoulders, as he folds his hands and kneels? Is it something you want your granddaughter to cuddle next to on chilly Sunday mornings to open her ears and eyes to your life lessons, to try them with her family who will pass them to their family, to reassure her spirits when life gets cloudy, to believe in herself the way you believe in her?

Consider putting together a word picture that may spark a "why" for your family legacy. Use metaphors and analogies to get your ideas across.

> *I want my family cathedral to be a lighthouse. Amid life's storms, I want it to be a beacon of hope. Amid the darkness of distress, I want it to illuminate truth through life experience. In life's tranquility, I want it be a place of rest and enjoyment – a place to listen and pause.*

*I want my family cathedral to be a coffee shop . . . a place where we can have authentic conversation – where laughter fills the air and big smiles abound. I want to sit around a fireplace and allow the glow of our family's stories to soak into our faces.*

*I want my family cathedral to be an urban neighborhood with neighbors stopping by the stoop not to be nosy, but to laugh and hold each other up.*

*I want my family cathedral to be a spring meadow blossoming with abundant assortment of wildflowers where whimsical stories – alive, raw, taut and brightly colored – bring smiles to faces.*

*I want my family cathedral to be a tree with deeply rooted stories passed from generations to nourish us, with trunk rings marking the growth through fire and drought, plentiful sunshine and abundant water. I want our family tree to be a place to rest in the shade of multigenerational lessons.*

*Your design needs a blueprinted plan.* Your family will choose their own path in life; the path inevitably leads to a destination. Your narrative provides the foresight for them to plan the right path choices. What are the choices and pursuits you want your children and grandchildren to make as teens, young adults, young professionals, newlyweds, parents? You want the kind of family narrative that illuminates how to master the huge jump from backpack to briefcase; or a narrative that engenders hope for your unemployed, depressed son; or a narrative that copes with the hurt of an unloved spouse; or teaches humility when you are ascending professional mountains.

We were made to dream. We are made to tell our story. There is glory to your life. So many stories and especially epics always harken back to legend and myth and things of the past. The origin myth of your family describes your family's folklore and their inextricable existence. You have a story to tell that starts with a vision for your family.

Isn't it true that your vision – for your family, for your marriage, for your kids – still makes your heart swell with anticipation and elation and possibility? Legacy, like cathedral building, isn't just about laying stones, but molding and shaping your family's future according to a grand design. While you inevitably enter and exit life stages, the spirit of your vision and the constancy of its calling is perpetual. Your family vision may be dormant after years, but it's not dead. Dust it off. Grab ahold of it. Pursue it. It's probably not tucked neatly inside your head, but clamoring inside your heart. Don't shrink it down based on how you see the size of your vessel. The great size and splendor of the cathedral was typically out of proportion to the town itself. Let your intrepid vision pull forward a future you desperately want for your family.

*Dear Kylie's girls,*

*I still remember the day that your mum phoned me and I heard the words "I have cancer." At first I thought I hadn't heard right. We were both in our early thirties at the time, starting families, looking to the future, proud of what we were achieving and discussing if we would finally get a tiny artful tattoo to celebrate our 40th since we chickened out when we turned 30. Never in my wildest dreams did I ever think that she would not survive. Your mum was full of life, everyone's friend, everyone's shoulder to cry on and the most masterful party organizer. Even when she and your dad had very little, she managed to conjure up a memorable event full of laughter and community spirit.*

*And she was my best friend. The person I truly talked to, the person I could open up to and who helped me through so much, and the person who showed me how to have a relationship with God. All of which I've not been so good at since she's been gone. Above all your mum was a fabulous person who gave so much and was devoted to the two of you, your dad, and God. You all*

*kept her going, kept her fighting and kept her wanting to sur-*
*vive to see you perform in the kiddy Christmas concert, see you*
*achieve your next milestone, and to see the bulbs that she planted*
*bloom in the next season.*

*You were both so young at the time that she worried that you*
*would not know her. She asked me to keep her alive for you both,*
*to help you understand who she was – the good bits and the not-*
*so-good bits because that's how you truly know someone. Today I*
*watch you from afar and I know your life has moved on. I some-*
*times wonder how I can stay true to what she asked. But then*
*I know that just as God somehow keeps gently encouraging me,*
*one day when the time is right, you'll want to know more and*
*I will share this letter with you. We can talk about the endless*
*stories of your mum and hopefully she'll feel alive to us both, even*
*just in those moments. Love, Sam*

## 2.0 Quarry Questions

1. *What is the "why" of your legacy building? Write several statements*
   *or phrases in your Legacy Letters journal, then choose the three most*
   *important.*

2. *What is folklore in your family? What stories are more like myths*
   *that define the origins and existence of your family?*

3. *What dreams do you have for your family that are too big to fit in*
   *your head, but can only fit in your heart? What vision of your family*
   *makes your heart swell with excitement and joy? Is your vision big*
   *enough, bold enough, enduring enough? What distinguishes it from*
   *other buildings on the horizon?*

4. *What are the destinations you want for them? Are they on the right*
   *paths?*

5.  *What kind of man or woman do you want them to become? What impact do you want your family to leave on the world?*

6.  *What would give you a big smile when you are 100 years old looking into the eyes of your children, grandchildren or maybe great-grand-children? Now trace back from your vision . . . How does your vision become reality?*

7.  *Has the vision for your family started to unravel? If so, what do you need to do to start winding it back up? How could you ensure it doesn't start to unravel?*

*2.0 Legacy Letters*

1.  *Write a story about one element of the vision you have for your family. Let them see its boldness.*

2.  *Look at the destinations you desire for your family. Choose one and tell a story showing them how the "power of the path" determines their destinations.*

## 2. Without a firm foundation, everything crumbles.

Cathedrals were renowned for their stunning architecture and their decorative features – exquisite sculptures, stained glass, ornate frescos – not their foundations. It would be understandable to expedite the humdrum foundation to commence the construction of walls, columns, and vaulted ceilings. This would be to the demise of the entire structure. Ascending cathedrals demand deep foundations. It was common for foundations to go as deep as twenty-five feet or more underground. The weight of every stone, pew, sculpture, and molten glass rested on the soundness of the foundation. Constructing the foundation required skillful planning, deliberateness, diligence. The foundation consisted typically of a layer of clay, then a layer of small stones followed by foundation stones. The foundation often determined the stability or failure of the structure within centuries, decades, or even after just a few years. Deviations were especially noticeable when the roof was added. Expedient mortar mixing and impatient curing time triggered wall collapse. Slapdash moisture control eventually resulted in buckling columns. The cathedral foundation is more than just the substratum underpinning for the walls, the columns, the stained glass; it also forms the outline of the monolithic, cruciform shape.

Millions of cubic meters were excavated for the foundation. The stones for the foundation were different. They were chosen for their superior strength. Quarryman, barely paid better than an un-skilled laborer, identified the essential stones for the foundation. The quarryman's work often started before the site even opened. Imagine those laborers of the staid foundation determining the du-rability of the entire building generations later. There was nothing glorious about the profession of foundation construction except that every successive stone placed on top of it rested on the su-premacy of its soundness. Placed by generations of your family, the weight of your family legacy is determined by your foundation – the values, the beliefs, the lessons you hold sacrosanct. Dig deep. Deep foundations create resilience and robustness for the weight of thousands of story stones.

## Excavate first

Before you start placing stones, you need to dig. Pay attention to childhood memories – the imprinting from earliest experiences. They shaped you. You need to excavate the past and face it to start building the future. Loss, despair, shattered dreams, regret, contempt – you need to look for the seeds of your life dissatisfaction; you need to look for the source of your discouragement; you need to identify the nucleus of your distress. You need to explore why you're touchy or tempered about certain things; why you are estranged and irritated in relation-ships. It may be a little messy and uncomfortable. But it just may be what allows your family to avoid the traps, the dead-ends, the hurt.

When we fail to let go of the noxious past – the lies, the abandon-ment, the betrayal, the pain – it owns us. It repeatedly haunts us. It continuously hurts us. If we don't want our baggage carried into the next generation, then we need to deal with our past and liberate our lives from its power over us. How long will you let the negative past define you? How long will you let someone else's careless words or cruel actions control you? How long will you let the damaging past be carried into future generations? It's not that we are cavalier about dismissing the humiliation, the deep insecurities, the lies. But legacy stories that will stick with our family have less to do with the foreboding circumstances and more to do with your transformation and transcendence.

---

"Our lives are a collection of stories – truths about who we are, what we believe, what we come from, how we struggle, and how we are strong. When we can let go of what people think...we gain access to our worthiness – the feeling that we are enough just as we are, and that we are worthy of love and belonging."
—Brene Brown, Daring Greatly

---

Face the past for them. You will find sources of inspiration – patient love for grandpa when his mind receded; second jobs to provide for college education; unresentful and graceful love overshadowing piercing, spiteful words; moments on mountaintops after climbing from valleys. Your stories just may be what imparts your family with hope, with courage, with forgiveness, with love. In To Be Told, Dr. Dan Allender says, "We wrongly believe that we will be happy if we can escape the past. But without the past we are hollow and plastic beings who have only common names and conventional stories."

Make a life map depicted with a sideways "T" across the length of a blank piece of paper. Time is across the horizontal axis and emotion across the vertical axis. Break the horizontal axis into life stages: childhood (0–7 years), adolescent (8–12 years), teen (13– 19 years), young adult (20–27 years), maturing adult (28–40 years), middle age (41–55 years), second wind (56–75 years), elder wisdom (76+ years). The upper vertical axis represents positive feelings – joy, happiness, surprise, courage, loyalty, honor, caring, affection, kindness, charitable, giving, love, and dozens of other positive emotions that you value. Write them down so you can see them plainly. The lower vertical axis represents negative feelings – hurt, loss, abandonment, anxiety, depression, jealousy, sadness. Think about salient memories in each life-stage especially in your early years. Mark dots onto the page with a brief description representing each experience – use the horizontal axis to assign the time period and the vertical axis for your emotion. Gently explore your past with a trusted friend who will listen, but not judge. Encircle experiences together that are linked. Look for patterns and connections. Make sense of your current circumstances in light of your past. *Why do you behave this way under certain circumstances? Why do you think and feel this way? Why do you over-react when someone says . . .? What is similar about the negative emotions and positive emotions?* These are the stones from the quarry of your life experiences – your story starters.

## Imprinting foundations

Imprinting is an animal behavior term used to describe how parents shape their newborns. It occurs when innate behaviors (e.g., flying, hunting, camouflaging, swimming, building shelters) are manifested in response to learned stimulus from parents. Behavioral patterns are transferred from parents to children after brief exposures early in life. Mallard chicks follow their mother, the first moving stimulus, between thirteen and sixteen hours after hatching. A child learns who its mother and father are in the womb when the unborn baby starts to recognize its parents' voices. Our values and beliefs, our truths and convictions, our principles and behaviors, our hopes and ideals are imprinted onto our family and it shapes the generations to come. As kings go, so do kingdoms; as fathers and mothers go, so do families. When the family unit fails, societies fail. Like the stonecutter that permanently marks every stone with his initials, our behaviors, words and actions imprint our children and grandchildren.

*Dear Madison and Meadow,*

*I want to tell you a story about family values. We learn family values from our parents and other members of our family. In turn, when you grow up and have families of your own, I hope that you will teach your children and your grandchildren the same important values that my mommy and daddy (your great-grandparents) taught my brothers, sisters and me.*

*The story I want to tell you is a true story, a story about me and the way I grew up. Ever since I was about two or three years old, I can remember sharing my things (toys, clothing, food, my home, even my bed . . .) with children in need. It was nothing, to wake up in the morning and sometimes see a little girl or little boy whom I did not know. I was always happy to meet them and to share a smile and whatever I had with them. That's because if they came to my house, my mommy and daddy knew that they needed help. I would always say, "Good Morning. My name is Janessa. What's your name?" Sometimes they would look nervous or worried, but that would always change when I gave them a smile and said, "Are you hungry? Let's go find something to eat."*

*I know that you may think that it would be very hard to share the things that you have with strangers, but honestly, it is the best feeling in the world! Especially when you find out how much more <u>you</u> have compared to the very little other people have. Once, I was upset because a little girl broke one of my dolls that I loved . . . but my mommy quickly explained to me that she had never had a doll before, and that she did not know <u>how</u> to play with my doll. I felt so sorry and embarrassed after that, and I never forgot how important it is to share what we have with others! Love forever, Janny*

*Experiences imprint.* We all have dreams of becoming great parents. We shower tenderness on our newborns. We yearn to hear "mommy and daddy" from our infant's mouth or cheer for their first steps. We beam with pride as our toddlers tackle milestones like potty training, reading, or catching a ball. Children are pure potentiality. They learn to understand the world and behave by observing everything and everyone around them. It's how children learn character, how lessons are transferred. So if we are imprinting life lessons by our example, how dutiful are we in mirroring what we say? If parents teach their children to be honest and then contradict the lesson by lying to someone, such lessons will never take root. How conscious are we that our behaviors are on permanent display, even those unintended and obscured? If parents teach their children to be kind to others, yet they see us dress down a waitress for mixing up our order, can we expect them to emulate our behavior or our veiled words? I watched my mom care for Mrs. Shaw, a dear elderly widow living four row homes away in Philadelphia. At about four o'clock each day, Mom would walk up and check on Mrs. Shaw. Mostly they would chat about Philly nostalgia or gossip about neighbors; Mrs. Shaw relished the conversation as a break from her solitary life reading novels and watching game shows and soap operas all day. We would run to the corner grocery store a few blocks away to buy milk, bread, deli meat, and cigarettes for her then quaintly chat with her about school, the news or family gatherings. We would take plates of food to her during holidays – always counting Mrs. Shaw among the guests. She would gush with gratitude and excitement for Mom's home cooking. The first time I saw my mom cry was when Mrs. Shaw died. Her son came to our door unexpectedly one evening with flowers and told us how much his mom cherished the fellowship with our family. I'll never forget his choked words: "She felt loved by your family." Selfless giving especially to older people was imprinted on me. Often our behaviors are oblivious to us and we need someone or some experience to awaken us from our behavioral hypnosis. Look at your children's behaviors – you'll have a front row seat to the behaviors you are unintentionally imprinting.

"Hear O' Israel: the Lord our God, the Lord is one! You shall love the Lord your God with all your heart, with all your soul, and with all your strength. And these words which I command you today shall be in your heart. You shall teach them diligently to your children, and shall talk of them when you sit in your house, when you walk by the way, when you lie down, and when you rise up." Deut 6:4-7 (NIV)

Our family resembles us more than in appearance. When he does that, he looks just like you. When she says that, she sounds just like you. Every day we are subtly imprinting. Our words are digging the earth. Our actions are placing the foundation stones. I remember a time shopping with my boys when we weren't charged for an expensive item at the department store. My sons knew that the bill was lower than we thought because they were buying Christmas presents for Mom and every penny counted. I could sense their initial reaction – *wow, how lucky she forgot to charge us.* Until I politely told the clerk that there was a mistake. She gushed with thankfulness. I knew it was coming . . . no sooner than we walked outside the department store: "Dad, why did you tell her, we could have had that for free!" "Boys, when we say that we don't steal things, it doesn't mean only when people aren't looking or if you can get away with it. When I say we don't ever take something that's not ours, I just don't mean for kids. I mean for me too . . . adults included." Apprenticing your family in foundation building isn't just compliance to our rules, but the internalization of why behaviors matter, seeing firsthand how you apply them, practicing them with you. What behaviors do you want intentionally imprinted?

*Dear Baili and Kara,*

*I am encouraged by your spirit. Despite the struggle, lecture, punishment, and disappointed looks, I am encouraged.*

*As parents, your father and I have not always believed our teaching could ever break through the closed bedroom doors, the earphones, or the rolled eyes. Somehow it has. We grew up in a time of struggle but nothing compared to that of your grandparents and great-grandparents. We have shielded you from much of this, only allowing glimpses of their pain and suffering to come through for fear of discouraging your future, always doubting our choices.*

*On the day of this latest "twin telepathy" occurrence, I was convinced that our jobs as parents have been well done. Not for the novelty that something happened to you both around the same time presumably because you're twins, but because individually it became obvious that you have surpassed even the compassion thresholds of your parents. Baili, I could not have been more proud when you called me while I was traveling on business and you were in tears because of the pain you felt on encountering a homeless gentleman begging for a Gatorade and immediately rushed to help. Kara, I could not have been more proud when you returned from your school trip to the Netherlands and told me of the day you also argued with your teacher when you wanted to break from the group at McDonald's to share your meal with a homeless gentleman and lost your appetite because she tried to stop you, but you did it anyway. Later learning that both of these happened on the same day while you were separated by an ocean was cute and interesting. Mostly it was a pivotal moment of confirmation that I admire the people you are becoming more than you will ever know. I tell that story now with pride, not because you're twins, but because you are individuals that will make a mighty difference in our future, always mindful of those less fortunate. Love, Mom*

*Marriage imprints.* We need to provide an imprint for marriage from which children draw inspiration for a successful relationship. Do our children know what's "behind the scenes" as parents or spouses, or are our children forming their opinions of marriage based on media's twisted depiction where the half-life of relationships is two and a half episodes? In movies or television shows our children rarely see compromise and selflessness, respect and commitment, sacrifice and growth, devotion and care as stalwart characteristics of husbands and wives. Instead, relationships are portrayed as expedient – unfulfilled . . . flee, dismayed . . . detour, unexciting . . . exit. Children and young adults get the skewed impression that marriage is something akin to returning something to a department store if it doesn't fit. Husbands and wives are portrayed in Hollywood as optional accessories for successful thirty-somethings. Rhonda Kruse Nordin in <u>Fragmented Families</u> says, "Somehow, the generation before me (my parents) and the generation before them (my grandparents) – sporting a low divorce rate and now unheard-of rates of cohabitation and single motherhood – modeled marriage as a unique partnership with inherent privileges, responsibilities, meaning, and purpose. Marriage was valued as a channel for self-development, self-respect, pride, and integrity. I wanted to sit in a tree, kiss, fall in love, marry, and have babies – *in that order.*"

Based on what children see in our relationships, they form perceptions, draw conclusions, and configure semi-permanent beliefs and expectations about marriage. Dr. Judith Siegel's research shows that by the time they leave home at age 18, children recognize marriage as either "good" or "bad" and have resolved if it is something they want for themselves. Unfortunately, most marriages are not making a positive imprint on our children. *The National Longitudinal Study of Youth* (ages 15 to 18) found that only 38% of teens believe their parents are happily married. In <u>Nurture Shock</u>, Po Bronson states, "Children appear to be highly attuned to the quality of their parents' relationship. Spouses express anger to each other two to three times as often as they show a moment of affection to each other." Do our children see how two people who care about each other resolve differences and can work out issues in a calm way with affection? Dr. Mark Cummings at the University of Notre Dame found that children's emotional well-being and security are more affected by the relationship between the parents than by the direct relationship between parent and child.

*Dear Jonathan, Nicholas, and Rachel,*

*The best gift I ever received was from mom on our wedding day. We had been saving every penny we could to pay for our wedding and whatever surplus we had was saved for our move to Michigan for graduate school. But on our wedding day, Aunt Chrissy delivered a gift as I nervously paced the church floor with my groomsmen. It was a beautiful watch from Mom with a note expressing our eternal time together. My heart swelled. I cherish it to this day. It does more than keep time; it reminds me of that beautiful day, a lifelong commitment and the thoughtfulness of mom who is always giving in our marriage. Gifts are more than the things we receive; they are both a whisper and a megaphone from the generous heart of the giver. Love, Dad*

If we are our children's imprint for marriage – what do they believe about its goodness? Do they know how it can be so easy to love your wife? How she can take your breath away when she walks in the room? How you love holding her hand? How you adore his embraces and sitting together so your legs gently touch? Do they know how natural it can be to love your husband despite his silly idiosyncrasies? How he makes you laugh like no one else until your belly aches? Do they know what's behind your boyish expressions for her and your pet names for each other? How you bring out the best in each other and blend your styles, your talents, your personalities? Do your children know how you share a dream about them? Do they know that feelings and intimacy aren't always euphoric, but honor and respect and devotion and love have knotted you together? Do they know your marriage requires hard work – sharing time and money, chiseling your hardened ego, watching sports that seem mindless but cause him to cheer, listening deeply, handling housework when you are tired, owning mistakes, watching movies that bore you but captivate her? Do they know that conflict is inevitable, that avoidance isn't the solution, but caring enough to compromise, to fulfill? Do they know how hard you cried every morning in the shower and evening on your pillow as she battled cancer? Do they know your secrets to a successful marriage – to compliment and apologize, to listen intentionally, to hold hands, to work at it, to accept imperfection, to serve unsolicited, to say "I love you" over and over again. Be overt about your marriage – tell them the why behind the what. Let them see it for what it is . . . beautiful, entrusted, complicated, magical, tiresome, enchanting, real.

*Quarry Questions 2.2*

1. *What behaviors do you need to intentionally imprint? What behaviors have you unintentionally imprinted? Make two columns in your Legacy Letters journal, one for behaviors you want to imprint and one for questionable behaviors you may be unintentionally imprinting, and then list as many of each.*

2. *What are the behind-the-scenes marriage characteristics you want to reveal to your family? What are the detours and dead-ends of marriage you want your family to avoid? Make two columns, one for the desired characteristics and one for the dead ends, and list as many of each.*

*Legacy Letters 2.2*

1. *Look at your list of intentionally and unintentionally imprinted behaviors and pick one to illustrate in a story. Be authentic and vulnerable in order to truthfully depict the desired characteristics as well as the dark side of behaviors you want your family to avoid.*

2. *Look at your list of marriage characteristics and pick one to write a story.*

*Stories imprint.* Kids live up to the stories we tell. When my kids were younger I'd lay in bed with them, and we would talk about their day. I artfully identified any hints of ego bruises, hurt feelings, poor decisions, joyful moments, or wish-I-could-do-it-over mistakes. Then I'd tell a story. *Their* story with them as the main character, personalized and embodied with "hints of realness" from their day. Some stories would be adventurous – camping, kayaking, hiking – or fun like birthday parties or sleepovers. Some would illuminate their giftedness in singing and dancing, cooking and writing, engineering and inventiveness. Some would highlight learning experiences like always protecting our little sister and mom, or feeling left out and lonely, or learning how to forgive, or the unforeseen consequences of stealing, or the boomerang effect of selfishness. Some would put current circumstances into perspective so they could see decisions across the horizon that spans more than a few days. Sometimes my kids would abruptly interrupt me in the beginning and tell me that's not what *really* happened. "It's just a story," I'd say and then I'd shape the clay with my hands.

> *One day there was a little boy named Nicholas who went camping with his brother Jonathan, sister Rachel, Mom, and Dad. We just finished setting up our tent when all of a sudden massive dark clouds and wind kicked up from the west. We all started shivering with the unexpected cold weather. While we huddled together shivering and uncertain what to do, Nicholas started collecting pieces of wood to build a fire. He took some flint and a cotton ball from his satchel and began creating sparks until at last one caught the cotton ball on fire. We cheered! What a clever boy – so well prepared! Before we knew it, Nicholas started a raging fire that warmed us to the bones from the chilly weather. He saved the day by being so prepared and thinking ahead. To celebrate we all had roasted marshmallows. Theeee eeeennnnnd.*

*One day there was a little girl named Rachel. She arrived at school and found a little girl teary-eyed on the playground. Everyone knows that Rachel has a big heart so she walked up to the girl whom she didn't recognize and asked her what was wrong. The girl was new to the school and missed her mommy. Rachel knew that feeling of being lonely, missing her mommy and feeling a little nervous at a new school. Rachel held her hand and walked her into her classroom. Rachel told her that she will be her friend and to meet her every day at the swings on the playground before school. "What is your name?" said Rachel. "Elizabeth," she said. "Wow, that's my middle name!" Elizabeth was comforted by Rachel's big encouraging smile and happiness in her eyes. Elizabeth gave Rachel a big hug. That was two years ago and they have been friends ever since then. Theeee eeennnnnd.*

Making kids the central figure of the story captures their attention and imagination. When we do, we are providing for them another vantage, the vantage of an experienced master builder. Your stories can use hindsight to create foresight. Storytelling allows our values to creep into the relevance of their everyday lives not through rules but through relationships. They can see how choices have real benefits and consequences. They "grow up to" moral decisions in the story. They see our family values come to life – how diligence, hard work, and patience matures and grows; how selflessness and generosity benefit the giver as much as the receiver; how putting others first doesn't always mean you are last; how faith and goodness prevails but not usually in the way we imagine. During weeks of tension between my son and daughter, one night with my son's head on my chest, I told him a story about the importance of being a big brother to his little sister. I *showed* him in an imagined story how he mattered more to his sister than he was aware. How she listens intently to him, follows him around the house, waits for him before choosing her ice cream, shares her cookies with him, talks to her friends about him . . . and is crushed when his words are hurtful. I showed him in stories how his decision to believe in her at a young age shaped her and made a difference decades later in her life. Wide eyed and proud, he turned a page and began writing a new chapter in their relationship. The next morning, he told me how he walked into her room later that night and told her how he was going to be a better big brother and best friend for her.

What makes up the foundation for your family? What are sacrosanct values and virtues? Uncompromising marks of character? Beliefs?

> *A (family name) always . . . {makes and keeps promises? Puts others before self? Respects/honors/cherishes women (especially moms and sisters)? Expresses gratitude? Is positive and encouraging no matter the circumstances? Will persevere because of her faith? Is self-disciplined? Humble and gentle? Compassionate to all}*

> *A (family name) never . . . {shaken by flattery or criticism? A gossiper behind someone's back? Arrogant? Ungrateful? Untruthful? Too proud to apologize}*

The foundation isn't magnificent. It hasn't exquisite ornateness. It isn't what visitors implore to see. But it is omnipotent. Build your foundation deep.

*Dear Madison and Meadow,*

> *How blessed we are that you have taken your rightful places among the many strong, courageous, and beautiful women who have been born into our circle of "family!" It is both wonderful and miraculous that you both show, even at this very early age, the purity of spirit, determination, and curiosity that enabled our family to overcome some of life's most challenging obstacles. Though your great-grandparents struggled to raise six children faced with the challenges of war, near poverty, racism, and chronic illness, they were able to teach us the true value of "family." Our parents demonstrated the power of love, dedication, and service.*

*We learned these lessons as we observed how they lived their lives and how they treated other people. You see, little ones, these lessons were reinforced as we observed how our parents became community leaders in the effort to support families of children with sickle cell anemia. They were most generous with their time, resources, and kindness to families, such as them, who were raising children born with this disease. They never abandoned this service, even after the loss of both of their own children to the disease. We were blessed to have parents who taught us by their example. Our parents, your great-grandparents, taught us that we were all born with unique talents and gifts that are meant to be used to improve our lives and the lives of others. They truly believed in love, self-determination, and service. I am so proud to say that we are still living the legacy of our parents by carrying on the same traditions that we were taught. I feel very confident that you both will also embrace this legacy and become strong, loving women of service because you are surrounded by parents and grandparents who love you and who also embody the traits that have enabled our family to endure. With love, Aunt Pat*

## 2.3 Quarry Questions

1. *Make a list of the sacrosanct values, character traits and beliefs you want imprinted with permanence on your kids and grandkids? Next to each write why they are so sacred to you.*

2. *Fill in the blank (no need to settle on a single answer): A (your family name) always . . .*

3. *Fill in the blank: A (your family name) never . . .*

4. *Make a list of as many story headings that demonstrate each value in (1) above.*

*2.3 Legacy Letters*

1. *What stories about your ancestors need to be told because their relevance has timeless significance?*

2. *What stories have been passed down the generations like family parables? You may not have the story perfect, but write what you know and have other family members shape it.*

3. *Tell them a story as if you are virtually snuggled next to each other sharing a cup of coffee in a cozy chair about one of your sacrosanct values or virtues in (1) above.*

4. *Give an example of each family value in action with a story about a family member. Start it with:*

   *"Let me tell you about a time when . . ."*
   *"Let me tell you what (insert value or virtue) looks like . . ."*

## Foundations provide resilience

Resilience in ecology and sociology is framed as *the capacity of a system, enterprise, or a person to maintain its core purpose and integrity in the face of dramatically changing circumstances.* Booming storms, crushing snow loads, toppling gales, and vacillating temperatures assaulted the handicraft of the cathedral worker toiling under extreme conditions. With the proper design and preparation, your family can withstand life's inevitable storms because your foundation provides resilience.

Tolerance and robustness in ecosystems can be strengthened with disturbance. Fire is a disturbance that creates resilience in forests. Fire is rarely catastrophic; renewal starts almost immediately. Ecosystems with fire history typically are more resilient than ecosystems that have never experienced fire. That's because one of the major determinants of fire is massive accumulation of detritus (dead wood) – fallen limbs, rotting trees, desiccant leaves. When the rate of detritus accumulation is greater than the rate of growth of living matter, the ecosystem is vulnerable. Fire is a counterbalancing source of regeneration, a temporary setback that sparks new growth. Fire releases an abundance of carbon-rich organic material and nutrients for the soil locked up in the detritus. Fire is harmful, but it usually doesn't destroy trees. What fires have unleashed something latent inside you? Fire temperatures open up the protected seeds that are dormant under normal conditions. Fire makes some nutrients more available by altering the soil pH and mineralizing them. Just imagine the grand design – seeds of renewal are only released under the intense heat of fire.

Adversity awakens something inside us. It can unexpectedly arrive in numerous forms – health, addiction, prodigal children, divorce, debt, abuse, unemployment, infidelity, crime – and it's always unwelcome. But adversity is an essential element of our narrative because it causes us to grow and stretch. Dave Allender in To Be Told puts it so well: "Even when tragedy has nothing to do with physical death, it still involves a form of death in the shattering of shalom or harmony. A divorce is a death. Sexual abuse is a death. Betrayal in a relationship, the loss of a job, conflict in a marriage, an auto accident, an illness, loss of meaning or hope or joy – all are forms of death. Death lies at the heart of all tragedy and at the core of every personal narrative." Sometimes the riptide of tragedy and loss can pull us under, gasping for air, far from shore, panicked. The adversity in your life has a purpose – use it to rescue them.

*Dear Cole, Peyton, and Walker,*

*When your dad wanted a divorce and moved out, I was so hurt and angry. I went through so many thoughts and emotions. It was like I was on an emotional rollercoaster that I couldn't stop. It's funny that in the movies and tabloids, divorces happen all the time and society portrays it as no big deal. Yet, it is a huge deal and the pain it causes to each person, the kids, friends, and family is deep and lasting. While I would never wish what we*

*went through on anyone, I am actually thankful that it hap-
pened because I learned a lot. I just want to share one with you.*

*Goodness: "And we know that God causes all things to work to-
gether for good to those who love God, to those who are called
according to His purpose" (Romans 8:28). Even when it seems
like nothing good can come of a situation, something will. It
would have been so much easier for our dad to stay on the path
he was on than to come back, apologize and ask to put our family
back together again. Admitting mistakes and making amends
takes a lot of courage and humiliation. It is not for wimps!*

*Our re-marriage to each other is so much better than the first.
We've learned to communicate, express our feelings, listen, respect and validate each other's feelings, show love in the way that
the other person feels loved, and reprioritize where our time and
energy is spent. Could we have gotten to this point another way?
Maybe, but I have my doubts. What we went through made us
stronger, wiser, more humble, and better individually and as a
couple. I am so thankful your dad and I have a new relationship,
stronger marriage, and that our family was restored. Love, Mom*

Resilience is deeply embedded in living things, in all of us. We can't
change our tragedies or eliminate the characters propelling them, but
we can tell our stories of resilience to encourage our family to rise
up, not give up. What if we found purpose in our tragedies? Not that
they were meant to happen, but what if they helped someone else deal
with similar adversity? What if your hardship gave someone the shove
to second guess, to pause, to break the cycle of dysfunction? What if
your story of survival gave someone hope to continue? What if your
foresight gave someone the confidence to "see it through" because renewal awaits? What if your survival gave someone the nudge to write
a new story in their life? What if your story unlocked a beautiful seed
that had been hidden for so many years? Generations of your family

aren't familiar with adversity, but they can consider it the source of something good because of you. They can see the trials that matured you, strengthened your character, grew your faith. In your stories they can find themselves strong enough.

*Dear Samantha and Al,*

*Years ago your Nana had a stroke. Strokes incapacitate parts of the brain. She lost some of the vision in her left eye; her temperature regulation was affected (that's why in their home with 77-degree weather outside the heat was on inside); she communicates awkwardly – when she says girls, she means boys; when she says she wants milk, that's OJ. It's different, it can be difficult, but she's here with us and we are so very grateful. When neurologists look at her brain scans they tell us she shouldn't be alive let alone be highly functioning. Only the perfect surgeon could have rewired Nana's brain – yes, He did. She's changed in another way – she's so much more lovable and sweet. It's not that Nana was a bad person, but sometimes crabbiness and nastiness and hurtful words wounded your mom especially when there was alcohol consumed. But after her stroke she was delightful, cheerful and her desire for alcohol vanished. Her sometimes cutting words were replaced with healing words. Unexpectedly, she would charmingly exclaim . . .*

*"You are such a wonderful mother."*
*"You are so beautiful today."*
*"How did I miss you all these years?"*
*"You are just wonderful!"*
*(To me) "Do you know how lucky you are to have her?"*

*So tense memories faded and new experiences replaced them. Sometimes I'll look over at Mom and see her stand in amazement, holding back the tears. When I see Nana smile, take ahold of Mom's hand, and look her in the eyes and say, "Oh, I love you so much," well, it takes my breath away. Sometimes the forest fires in life sprout new growth. They can be tragically painful and devastating, but they can also spark a new beginning. Love, Dad*

Isn't it true that you need to fail a little to learn a lot? Isn't it true that some of your most compelling life lessons were at the bottom of the pit, not at the top of the mountain? When you fight you learn something deeper about yourself. When you struggle or toil or thrash, you emerge with deeper convictions, stronger character, tested values, persevering faith.

What's the internal script that your family tells themselves in crisis, in failure, in success, in pain, in injustice, in celebration, in happiness? That script isn't determined by their education or their talents or their network or their profession; the script comes from you. Your legacy lessons can imprint resilience for your progeny. When we enter tragic circumstances, we can only see an endless road. Darkness. Your stories can be light for them. Tell them a story about your teenage heartache – how you felt the pull to abandon your moral guardrails, how you stayed true to yourself, but lost your love and ended up . . . better. Tell them about winning your battle over a health crisis and how you ended up . . . better. Tell them about suffering through a team work crisis and how your strength of character pulled them out of the disaster . . . better. Tell them about your sister who held you up when your partner's infidelity crushed you and how her assurance and intentional listening made life for you . . . better. Tell them about a different side of your grandpop who didn't pay off your mounting debt, but helped you find a job to pay it off. Tell them how you did it, all of it, standing tall. Tell them how you did it on your knees. Tell them that the roots of your growth emanated from adversity.

It's not the easy life that capture's our attention and causes us to lean in and listen closely so we can learn. In the midst of life's storms, you need your foundations to run deep so your family cathedral doesn't crumble.

## 2.4 Quarry Questions

1. *Write in your Legacy Letters journal about the fires in your life that seeded something anew and created resilience in you.*

2. *We naturally shy from circumstances that are painful, but in doing so we accumulate detritus. The detritus in our lives can take many forms – unresolved character flaws, unexpressed gratitude, unforgiveness and resentment, parched relationships, hurtful words, overscheduled lives, skewed self-perceptions that have become self-fulfilling. Make a list of the detritus in your life that you need to release and burn as the dead past.*

3. *The bottom is different for all of us. When have you seen the bottom, felt the bottom, languished at the bottom? Tell us how you were rescued; how you climbed and crawled out? Who helped you out?*

## 2.4 Legacy Letters

1. *Tell stories of how the temporary fire of painful circumstances in (1) or (3) above ultimately sparked new growth and opened new seeds in your life. What did you learn about yourself? How did it make you stronger?*

2. *What are some life experiences that can inspire your family to remain steadfast and resolute to values amid the storms? Retell some life experiences when you were tested, vulnerable, shaken, but your unfaltering values, implacable character or faithfulness to your beliefs prevailed.*

3. *Write a letter to a family member whose example has inspired a spirit of resilience in you.*

## Plumbing the heart

A plumb line is a simple but accurate "vertical level" tool. Used since ancient times, a plumb line consists merely of a line and a weight of some sort, at first just a stone, but later a weight made from lead. Manuscript illustrations show masons using a simple level consisting of a straight edge with a raised circle from which a plumb line with a weight hung. A square and a compass completed the master builders' tools for assessing alignment, position, and evenness. These tools were so important in construction that they have survived into the modern day as symbols of the mason's trade. Master masons were constantly checking with the level for horizontal exactness and the plumb for vertical precision. This was called plumbing. Any distortions horizontally or declinations vertically most certainly caused structural issues over time.

---

"We don't want to be someone's project; we want to be the desire of their heart." — John Eldredge, Waking the Dead

---

*Getting our family's heart right is a plumb line for a sound foundation.* From the heart springs creativity and fortitude, courage and conviction, faith and hope, compassion and love. "Above all else, guard your heart, everything you do flows from it" (Proverbs 4:23). Nothing can be as precious as getting our family's hearts in the right place. Not big salaried careers or prestigious appointments or vacation homes or grade-skipping smarts or taller-than-your-kids trophies. We need our family to *see their worth* and acceptance – independent of worldly performance; we need our family to *feel* our absolute love independent of circumstances. There are no win-loss columns with absolute love; it is a no-strings-attached bond between moms and dads and their children, grandparents and their grandkids that cultivates heart health. My son remembers with intricate detail how I put him to bed as a little boy. He explained it to me this way . . ." I loved getting under the cold covers and having you rest your hand on my head then my heart. You'd say a prayer with soft words that made me sleepy. Then you'd warm my insides with a big hug. Sometimes it felt so good, like candy, I'd ask for another one." Are we preparing hearts as the foundation of our family's cathedral? Are we plumbing our family's hearts to ensure they are upright, principled?

*Dear Rachel,*

*You had been training twice a week for months with girls in your elementary school and your mom as a coach for a 5K race. You asked me to run with you. So on race day with thousands of other girls and parents, we ran. The race was exhilarating, and I enjoyed watching you take in the music and cheering crowds on the streets. But between mile 1 and 2, you hit a wall. You didn't just slow down, you stopped; you felt defeated and wanted to give up. But then you asked me to start running again with you with five simple words that uplifted me: "Can you hold my hand?" With misty eyes I held your hand tightly and we crusaded through the streets of Atlanta. In that moment you thought that you needed me, but in a different way I needed you just as much. Few things that year were more memorable than running alongside you as we crossed the finish line together. I will always be there to hold your hand. Love, Dad*

Many of us unintentionality transfer our perfectionist tendencies to our family with the right intentions, but with unintended consequences. Incessantly performing, pleasing and proving can erode self-esteem. When your son or daughter looks in the mirror, what do they see? Is the image distorted, pleasing, critical? Without your voice of encouragement, an inner critic emerges with a rehearsed phrase – "never good enough." "Never good enough" creates a void. "Never good enough" calcifies and hardens. "Never good enough" fears failure. Countless kids and grandkids may never learn their true strengths and how to serve them up to the world because of "never good enough."

*Dear David,*

*I will never forget the day I took you to Firearm Safety Class after seeing how guns were mis-portrayed in your video games. Watching you gain a more realistic perception was important, seeing you fire a real gun for the first time was cool, but hearing you on the drive home call it "The best father-son day ever!" was priceless. It took us 13 years and several failed attempts (baseball, tennis, soccer) but that day opened the door to us discovering competitive shooting as our common interest and opportunity to spend enjoyable quality time together.*

*Another thing I will never forget is the first time you beat me in a Light Rifle Match. A couple of years into our hobby I remember feeling a little disappointed in you—I thought you should be more dedicated and practice more frequently. I was also a little disappointed that you were still satisfied with the inexpensive second-hand Savage 22 rifle I bought you soon after the safety class. So using my advanced fatherly wisdom I decided the situation was a good teachable moment. I bought myself an Anschutz 22, the fanciest high end brand on the market. And I started going to the indoor practice range 2-3 times more often that you.*

*When the new Light Rifle season began I was all set demonstrate the benefits of drive, superior equipment and practice. But you proceeded, with your pawn shop Savage 22 and your once-a-month practice regimen, to beat me several times and set several national records during that season. More importantly, while I was pressuring myself to live up to my elevated expectations, you were relaxed and having fun. That season was indeed a teachable moment—but as it turned out you were the teacher and I was the pupil. Little is more rewarding in the life of a father than the first time being "beaten" by his son—and in this case it wasn't just in shooting ability. I am so very proud of you! Dad*

Our family needs to feel bonded together and belonged to. They need to know that they matter to you. They need to see that they fit, that they aren't a mistake or a hassle or an outlier. They may be a carpenter and you may be a quarryman, but you both long to build with your distinct giftedness. Our family needs to feel accepted. No one is ever too old to feel the joy of acceptance from their parents. This is true for youngsters as well as adult children. We never outgrow the adulation of mom or dad, grandma or grandpa saying, "I'm proud of you" or "you are special to me" or "I'm incredibly grateful to have you as a son" or "I'm blessed to have you as my daughter" or "you are a great mom." It's a lifelong desire of our hearts – to be noticed by mom and dad.

> *Dear Jonathan, Nicholas and Rachel,*
>
> *When I met your mom, it was love at first sight. But when you were born, it was love before first sight. I love you so much! It's not because of anything that you do, but just because you are you. You are special. Rachel – caring and considerate of others before yourself, you have a heart of gold; your hugs make me smile and my worries melt away. Nicholas – you are so witty and clever; always knowing how to blanket our family with laughter; you are a special big brother to your sister. Jonathan – you are diligent and dependable; you help without asking. We belong to each other. I am yours and you are mine. We may be disappointed or frustrated with each other on our journey together (I know you will of me) because we are imperfect, but I want you to confidently know that I love you and I've got your back. I've had a lot of titles in my life, but "Dad" brings me the most joy. When the nurse placed you in my arms for the first time, I remember softly whispering in exhilaration – "he's mine!" "she's mine!" And I'd proudly say those words over and over again throughout my entire life. Love, Dad*

*A strong heart braves life.* In life our family will feel hurt, will experience fear, will feel grief, and will experience joy and exhilaration. When they feel accepted and loved, they will live with their hearts open, not closed – willing to forgive, willing to be courageous, willing to be a little embarrassed, willing to give, willing to trust. In the fog of life, we don't see things as clearly as we ought to and it's not easy to see what's happening to those we love. That's why we need to plumb frequently – is your family's heart in the right place?

*2.5 Quarry Questions*

1. *Think about each member of your family. Plumb their heart . . . In what ways is it in the right place, not in the right place?*

2. *What circumstances easily cause your family's heart to be skewed and off-balance? Can you see how it adversely affects the values you treasured in Quarry Questions 2.3?*

*2.5 Legacy Letters*

1. *Write a story to your family about a time when your heart was "off-center." What important lesson do you want your family to learn?*

2. *Write a story when you were glad your heart was in the right place. When you heart was fulfilled? When your heart practically leapt from your chest.*

## 3. Stories are the stones. Relationships are the mortar.

At the turn of the twentieth century, some French children made an incredible discovery in the Pyrenees Mountains – drawings of extinct animals in caves. The 35,000-year-old paintings on the walls of the Lascaux Caves are our earliest recorded evidence of storytelling. Stories brought the vividness of events to those who did not participate in the hunt, flood, and voyage. Storytelling has been used by cultures and clans across the world for thousands of years. Anthropologists tell us that one determinant of flourishing, enduring societies and ephemeral ones is the ability to transfer wisdom, lessons, and knowledge from one generation to the next. Storytelling may be the oldest form of influence in human history. Every major world culture and civilization has used or continues to use story to transfer knowledge, teaching, morality, virtues, and values. In some African cultures, stories are so integral to the people that every question is answered by a story. Through storytelling, Celtic, African, Indian, and Native American tribes shared and preserved their early beginnings and paid tribute to their ancestry. With storytelling came cultural and community bonding. In Boys Adrift, Dr. Leonard Sax writes, ". . . [cultures that have lasted for hundreds or thousands of years] pass the rules for what is expected of mature adults from one generation to the next . . . These cultures – like almost every other enduring culture of which we have detailed knowledge – pass this information from one generation to the next in gender-specific communities. Women teach girls what is expected of adult women in their community. Men teach boys."

---

"If a picture is worth a thousand words, then a story is worth a thousand assurances." — The Story Factor

---

We have today because of what those before us told us, modeled for us, instilled in us. How much do our children, grandchildren, nieces, and nephews really know about their family who rose above racism or immigrated to another country starting from scratch or protected our freedom with valor in armed service through wars? Not through the pages of history textbooks will we find their indelible mark, but through the stories you tell. Storytelling can be the golden threads of beautiful wisdom that weaves our family together through multiple generations.

*Rya, Tali and David,*

*Grandma Rosie was accepted to college just as the Great Depression hit the United States. Although it was very unusual for women to attend college, this was Grandma Rosie's dream. She loved to learn and was brilliant. Instead Grandma Rosie stayed home. She met and married Grandpa Roxie and had three daughters. Grandpa Roxie died when Grandma Rosie was 40 and left her very little money and no career. Grandma Rosie's lifestyle changed dramatically. She moved herself and my mom into her cousin's house. They shared a room. Grandma Rosie worked retail to pay for her daughters' college. She never remarried and died at the age of 83. After telling this story, Grandma Rosie would then add the moral which I now practice: "Never rely on a man to support you financially. Women need to be able to take care of themselves. As a result, you will marry out of love, not need." With love, Mom*

*Mark your Ebenezers.* The Philistines were about to attack the Israelites. Surrounded, outnumbered, terrified, dire. "Samuel cried out to the Lord on Israel's behalf and the Lord answered him.... The Philistines drew near to engage Israel in battle. But that day the Lord thundered with loud thunder against the Philistines and threw them into such a panic that they were routed before the Israelites.... Then Samuel took a stone and set it up between Mizpah and Shen. He named it Ebenezer saying, 'Thus far the Lord has helped us.'" (1 Samuel 10, 12). Samuel publicly dedicated a monument to God, a reminder of His provision and protection. The busyness of life can fade our memories; dampen the realness of blessings, the goodness in our lives, the defining moments that marked you. Take the time to erect Ebenezer stones (translated "Stone of Help") in the form of stories. When you take the time to erect them, the story-monuments endure for your progeny. Maybe even physically collect stones, hold them as tangible remembrances. Ebenezers do more than explain your journey, they explain you and your faith more deeply. What are Ebenezers in your life?

The Pawnee and Lakota Native American tribes carry artifacts from the tribe's past in a pouch called a sacred bundle. Each artifact is associated with a rich and meaningful story that is shared among the tribe. The stories were told so often that every member of the tribe could recall and repeat them to their families. What artifacts would be in your family's sacred bundle? What stories accompany each artifact?

---

"Most of the time, you won't be present when the people you want to influence make the decisions, choose the behaviors you were hoping to influence, or both. You don't have much, if any, formal authority over them and you cannot easily predict the specifics of the situation in which they might find themselves, so how do you get them to do what you want?"
— The Story Factor

---

Storytelling magically involves the mingling of the teller and listener that transcends time, sharing not just words and plots but emotions and experiences. When we invented stories, we invented heroes and villains and we celebrated ordinary men and women doing incredible acts of surpassing kindness, boundless bravery, undaunted courage, relentless love, unwavering moral decision-making. Everyone wants the opportunity to express their story and deep down everyone wants to be proud of their lives. Stories give our struggle meaning. This is the vein that runs through your story.

Stories captivate our family by addressing perplexing questions. Family rules can't explain paradoxes in life, but stories can. Growth through desperation. More from less. Finding fullness from emptiness. Renewal from fire. Stories help us to answer *yes* and *no* to complex questions without being wishy-washy. Stories nudge them to make wise decisions. Stories make spirituality real. Stories imprint your values and your voice so they can spontaneously recall them in their everyday lives.

*Dear Jonathan, Nicholas, and Rachel,*

*I learned an incredible lesson during my first few years working. I had been assigned to a high priority project as a lead scientist. We were developing flushable/biodegradable products to reduce the environmental impact of our disposable products. To evaluate the "flushability" of certain products, I needed to test dozens of materials and product designs. So I build a toilet stand with several different kinds of toilets and began flushing experiments. (Yes, Dad started his illustrious career flushing toilets. When I told you that no job is under you, I really meant it.) I asked for a technician to assist me in literally hundreds of these flushing experiments every day. Tracy came with a reputation as a lazy technician and a recovering alcoholic. Several people would roll their eyes when I mentioned her name . . . "She can't think for herself, but she's a great pair of hands." So I treated Tracy based on the perceptions of others. She would often make observations during countless daily flushes. I'd politely hear her, but never really listen after all I had an engineering degree and she had a high school education. I'd just ask her to "just give me the data." After a few months of working with Tracy, I grew to respect her unbelievable work ethic. She enjoyed what she did and she never complained about repeating the same mindless task – flushing and recording – over and over all day. One day I actually listened to one of Tracy's many astute observations. She revealed an incredible insight that became the foundation for the rapid development of the project. "I have been telling you this for a while," she politely chided me as I thanked her. I was so embarrassed. I had dismissed her contribution – her ideas and insights and analysis – for months. Today her fingerprints are on a product used by millions of people across the globe. After*

*15 years as a lab technician, Tracy was promoted to a scientist based on her keen observations and hard work. She was so proud to tell her husband, kids, and grandkids! Tracy had potential for years, but no one ever gave her a chance and for months neither did I. Many years after I left that team, I received an invitation 750 miles away for Tracy's retirement party after working at Kimberly-Clark for 30 years. The note inside made me cry. Tracy thanked me for giving her a chance to prove her potential – to herself, her family and her company. She was retiring from K-C with the esteemed self-satisfaction of not just having worked for three decades, but contributing her gifted best.*

*Never let other's perceptions create a veil for you to see someone for who they really are. Give everyone a chance; then give them a second chance. Humble yourself and watch for the greatness in everyone. That greatness exists but you need to look for it. Maybe, just maybe you'll have the incredible privilege of helping someone shower the world with their gifted potential. And in the process, you'll be changed too. Love, Dad.*

*Stories provide depth and vividness.* Stories provide a context that often is overlooked in daily life. Stories can illuminate the color of character in an otherwise monochromatic image of relatives. When I would stay at my grandparents' house, I'd wonder why there would be dozens of boxes of toothpaste, toothbrushes, razors, shaving cream, bars of soap, shampoo, batteries, candles, matches. There weren't just a few extra items to avoid running out of the essentials, but an entire closet full of toiletries. My parents would chuckle and put aside the behavior as quirky. Until one weekend visit I remember listening to my grandparents for hours tell stories of the World War I era. First they spoke little about the war itself, but instead of the jubilant times post war – a time of possibility and resetting jobs, families, community. But with crackled voices they also spoke of austerity before and during the war and I could see desperation in their faces. They spoke of living with practically nothing, sacrificing "essentials" for the war and living with only hope. My grandfather served in WWI and my grandmother was alone living on meager wages having no certainty of future means for food, personal care items, money. Their story reframed the context of a closet full of personal care items from quirky to noble, from sales-priced inventory to a stockpile of preparedness. Later when I went to the grocery store with my grandmother and watched her buy even more bars of soap, I didn't see hoarding but vigilance for the unexpected austerity that surreptitiously marked a generation. Now alongside my affection and love, I added a deep regard for their sacrifice. Stories are a gateway for understanding, empathizing, humanizing.

---

It's possible to bend language at your will, to invest extraordinary amounts of effort and care to make words do what you want them to do. You may not have the resources or a physique or the connections that people who do other sorts of work have. But you do have precisely the same keyboard as everyone else. It's the most level playing field we've got." — Seth Godin

---

Your family has been investing years, decades, generations in the unseen foundation of your family cathedral. Look for the stories. What legacy stories are buried beneath passing conversations with your ordinary aunts and uncles, familiar grandparents, dull moms and dads? I was having a conversation with a cheerful 88-year old-woman who was thrilled to chat about golf. In just a few minutes of intently listening, I uncovered that she was one of the first women to play golf on a collegiate team . . . the only woman on the all-male team. She was a feisty and fearless pioneer for women in a game that enchanted her. She recalled with searing memory the magical putts and stalwart drives and mystical bunker shots; teasing male teammates who collapsed under pressure as she soared. With a warm smile she said,

"Thank you for making this a wonderful day. No one has ever asked me *why* I loved golf."

Take the time to probe deeper into the passing stories. Listen whole-heartedly with open ears and an open heart. Look for the concealed passion. The experiences of past generations – their hard lives, their remarkable reversals, their enduring love – made an distinct mark on your family. Tell us those stories. They add depth and contrast to the photographs of distant relatives who secretly forged a path for you. They shine abiding wisdom for you to see ahead.

*Rya, Tali, and David,*

*If you ever wonder how I became the woman I am today, you can look to stories that have been passed down to me about my family. Most of these stories are from before my time. However, they have a profound impact on who I am today. It gives me great joy to know that by passing these stories to you, like when Grandma and Pa were dating, they will shape who you are too.*

*Pa wanted a more serious relationship and didn't know how Grandma felt. Being a writer, he sent Grandma a letter with a flower and tree seeds. In the letter he asked Grandma, "Is our love like a flower or tree?" He described that a love like a flower is beautiful and admired by many. It blossoms, but eventually dies. A love like a tree has strong roots that hold itself up through good and bad times. It grows over time and provides for generations. Fortunately, Grandma replied, "Our love is like a tree," and they quickly they got engaged. Every year on their anniversary Pa would send flowers to Grandma with a note that says, "Flowers for our Tree." Hearing this story multiple times instilled in me the importance of creating a strong foundation of love and support for my family, first and foremost. With love, Mom*

*Stories linger and transcend time.* When we tell stories, it's more participatory than just telling our kids what to do. Stories are easily remembered because our brains affix deep memories to the engagement and the emotion. Situations may change, but the story is timeless and always seems to find relevance. A story may be remembered for a long time, but new depths of its meaning and significance are continuously discovered as you grow.

*Dear Jay, Chris, Andrew, and my nieces and nephews,*

*It was an early September Saturday morning when I heard the ringing of my blue princess phone in my bedroom. Feeling a sense of foreboding, I hesitatingly picked up the phone and heard the voice of my next door neighbor Delores. She told me in a rushed voice that my sister Mary Ellen and her best friend Nancy, her daughter, were in a car accident in New Jersey seventy miles away and we all had to go to the hospital to see them. I quickly bounced out of bed and ran into my mother's bedroom and relayed the news. We both dressed hurriedly and ran outside where my neighbors were warming up the car that would take us all to the hospital. We were all talking nervously in the car about the weather and odds and ends never even remotely suspecting what was ahead of us. When we got to the hospital, we were told to wait in a small room which was filled with lots of people. After a few minutes a doctor approached my mother and asked her name and my mom told him and then he said dispassionately that "Mary Ellen was dead" and my mother screamed and then collapsed. Then Delores our next door neighbor screamed: "What about Nancy?" and he once again in a deadpanned voice said, "Nancy is dead too." You see her VW beetle was hit by a drunken driver and she was thrown 100 feet from her seat in the car along with Nancy. Only one girl survived the accident.*

*Mary Ellen was generous of heart and spirit and had an infectious laugh and was always doing good for others. She was a character and a champion of the underdog as was my Dad so they had a unique relationship. The funeral and the celebration of both girls' lives were filled with wonderful stories from friends and family and the happy times that we spent together. It was a tremendous comfort to all of us especially my parents to see that their child was so loved and cherished. Thousands of people were present at both viewings and funerals which were held adjacent to each other. It was a time that I will never forget and the true beauty of the human spirit with family and friends who wrap their arms around during your time of need. My mom just wanted to talk about my sister all the time and my Dad couldn't talk about it at all and held his emotions to himself. So I was the one who my Mom poured her heart out to, and I listened day after day and month after month and for years really to all of Mom's thoughts, worries, stories, and concerns.*

*When we lose someone so young and so tragically in a family it is a wound that never heals and contrary to the popular saying, time does not heal all wounds. The pain never really goes away but remains like a dull ache in your heart. While my sister Mary Ellen didn't get an opportunity to have a family of her own she will never be forgotten in my own family as we speak about her and the wonderful memories we shared with her. The legacy of Mary Ellen and her gifts to the world will live forever in my memory. I hope by writing this letter that she will also be remembered by my children and their children who will when then pass on this story to their families. But most of all I hope they learn the lesson of family and how it is so important to be there for each other as there is no one else that cares about you as much as your family. Love, Mom*

*Stories penetrate cultural imprints.* While parenting will always be a primary influence for teaching our children, hidden assumptions and biases are creeping into their lives from peers and media. Po Bronson in <u>Nurture Shock</u> says, "We are inadvertently teaching our kids to socialize themselves . . . the average teen spends sixty hours a week surrounded by a peer group (and only sixteen hours a week surrounded by adults)." In the peer world the need for social status and acceptance is primal which is why physical and relational bullying, such as exclusion, withdrawing friendship, telling lies, or spreading rumors, is rewarded with peer status, awe, and influence. A study by the American Academy of Pediatrics in 2013 found that the average eight to ten year old spends nearly eight hours a day with a variety of media. Dr. Victor Strasburger, a professor of pediatrics at the University of New Mexico and author of the AAP study, says kids today are "spending more time with media than they are in school. They are spending more time with media than in any activity other than sleeping. You could make the argument that media have taken over the primary role of teaching kids from schools and parents in many cases . . . we are worried a lot of parents are clueless about their kids' media use and how to manage it appropriately." Dr. Cynthia Scheibe at Ithaca College found that 96% of all children's programming includes verbal insults and put-downs, averaging 7.7 put-downs per half-hour episode. Of the 2,628 put-downs the social scientists observed, in only 50 occurrences was the insulter reprimanded or corrected. For the remainder 84% of the time, there was either only laughter or no response at all.

Schemas are mental shortcuts of pre-conceived ideas and assumptions representing some view of the world so our brains can quickly process information. We don't think about brushing our teeth or driving to work or stopping at red lights or pouring the coffee – we are automated. We use schemas to rapidly organize new information or experiences using a framework from the past.

While we all develop schemas in our lives, they can cause us to passively accept behaviors and experiences as "normal." If we don't create appropriate reference points for our kids, then culture will create schemas for them. *Money equals your worth. Life is about winning. If you aren't happy, then quit. Me first.* Our stories have the potential to reframe the subtle biases and hidden assumptions that seep into our lives. A friend was having difficulty telling her twenty-something daughter that her boyfriend wasn't treating her with kindness and consideration. The daughter wanted her boyfriend to pick her up from the airport after a late-night flight because she was concerned about taking public transportation and couldn't afford a taxi. Her boyfriend has a favorite television show that night and the trip to the airport is 40 minutes away causing him to miss his show. Mom sees boyfriend as selfish and inconsiderate. Her daughter is confused because she would pick up her boyfriend if he was flying in late, but understands that it is an inconvenience on him. Reluctantly, she says, "Love means we are considerate of the other person's interests and feelings, right? I want to be considerate of something important to him. Love doesn't mean that someone has to do things for me. Mom, my generation . . . we need to be our own person and not rely on our partners for everything." How do you tell your daughter that she isn't being treated respectfully, selflessly, lovingly? Her frame of reference – the love of her life, culture, media shouts a schema that she has reluctantly accepted – *serving others in a relationship is an unnecessary hassle, we need to think about ourselves first, I need to do things for myself.* So Mom needed to change her schema. Preaching and finger-pointing wasn't going to work. The daughter may listen, but she'll tune out and filter Mom's words. Stories penetrate schemas. "Your dad would never treat me or you that way. Let me tell you a story about a time when he went out of his way for me." Followed by "let me tell you a time when he went out of his way for you." Followed by "let me tell you another story when he did something that just took my breath away . . ." Followed by "when I had cancer, *everything* was inconvenient . . . I could *always* rely on him certainly not because it was easy for him but because he is devoted to me." Delicately that schema was disassembled. Authentic stories cause us to rethink our hidden assumptions and poke holes in their illogic so that distorted images eventually come into focus.

*Dear Micaela, Cameron, Kelsey, Moriah, and Madison,*

*I don't like nursing homes very much. It's not that I don't like the elderly, or that I am not merciful. It's just that when I go to a nursing home, I am reminded so vividly that my life is just a "vapor," here today, and gone tomorrow.*

*A few years ago, I traveled with your grandfather to spend time with his mother. Both of my maternal grandparents had passed away before my tenth birthday. My paternal grandfather had passed away when my dad was only 17. So for most of my life, Rebecca Cameron Turner was my only living grandparent.*

*Now, grandma was over 90, suffering from dementia, a widow for more years than she had been married. Frail. Confused. When we met her in the lobby of her home, she recognized neither of us.*

*"You look familiar," grandma said to her son, my father.*
*"I am your son, Phil."*
*"No . . . that's not it. But you look like someone I know."*

*How could this be? This strong woman, my grandmother unable to recognize her son. Her sharp wit and dry humor had been turned to confusion and uncertainty.*

*We tried for a while to talk. We had traveled so far, and I had so looked forward to this moment. Now, I grieved that my expectations for my time with grandmother had been shattered. I asked myself, "Why hadn't I spent more time with her? Why hadn't I called more? Why hadn't I written more? Why had I been such a disinterested grandson?"*

*It was obvious she was getting more and more unsettled, and so we wheeled her back to her room and helped her into bed. My father said his farewells and headed out the door. As I turned to do the same, a small, frail hand reached out and grabbed mine.*

*"You're Michelle's brother aren't you?" Grandma asked.*
*"Yes," I said, shocked by the unexpected moment of clarity.*
*"You're going to be a pastor someday, aren't you?"*
*"Yes, Grandma. I already am."*

*"Then tell me, why can't I go home to see Jesus? And why can't I see Chuck (her husband) again? Why am I still here?"*

*"All I can say, Grandma" – still shaken by the clarity of her mind – "is that God is not finished with you yet. He still has a plan and a purpose for you."*

*"You are going to make a good pastor someday," grandma said, as a warm smile spread across her wrinkled face. With a squeeze of my hand, she gazed into my eyes and said, "I love you."*

*With that, she rolled over and lapsed back into the haze of confusion and uncertainty. But for just a moment, everything seemed to converge in a moment of unbridled joy and hope and peace and love. My expectations and my regrets all melted away at the chance to love and be loved. There is no greater experience!*

*I share this story with you so that you do not fail to do today what you may regret failing to do tomorrow. Live, love, and invest in people today, for we never know what tomorrow may hold. Joy can come in the midst of suffering. The real secret to life is not avoiding suffering, but rather finding the sacred in the midst of suffering. Love, Dad*

*2.6 Quarry Questions*

1. *Spend time deeply listening and probing for more insight beyond the "niceties" with parents, grandparents, aunts, and uncles. Perhaps probe with: When was a time you felt most vulnerable? Proud and on top of the world? Deeply cherished and loved? What did they experience but never want you to face?*

2. *Make a list in your Legacy Letter journal of schemas that you have reframed resulting in a dramatic change or defining moment for you?*

3. *What schemas do each of your family members have that need to be reframed?*

*2.6 Legacy Letters*

1. *Tell a story, or preferably multiple stories to reframe a family member's schema you wish to dismantle.*

2. *Write a story that provides vividness and depth to understand an element of your life? What stories are timeless even now after so many years have passed? What stories need to be told over and over again?*

**Relationships are the mortar**

Stories make us matter to each other. Relationships form the currency of our experiences; they flow between our stories and hold them together. Our stories are formed in the overlapping circles of relationships from our present and past.

Can you name the people who made an impression on your life?

Can you name three friends who helped you during rough patches in your life?

Can you name people who helped shape your character?

Can you think of people who accepted you for who you are and love(d) you with no strings attached?

Can you think of people who gave you a chance, who invested in you?

The mortar in the cathedrals took an exceptional amount of time to cure – weeks, months, years, decades. Curing needed the right conditions and the frigid temperatures, high humidity and lack of oxygen were deleterious. Mortar didn't just hold the finished stones together, but the structurally important twelve to eighteen inches of interior mix of stone and mortar between the inner and outer walls. Like mortar, our relationships need curing time – rival siblings bond over years; prodigal children inch their way home with time; sisters confide; brothers unite. What seems too wet to ever affix, over time conjoins and connects hearts. As the mortar cures, the relationships solidify.

---

"'Don't lose touch with the friends you value most, Bronnie. Those who accept you as who you are, and who know you very well, are worth more than anything in the end. This is a woman speaking from experience,' she insisted lightly, smiling at me through her illness. 'Don't let life get in the way. Just always know where to find them and let them know you appreciate them in the meantime.'"
— Bronnie Ware, The Top Five Regrets of the Dying

---

When the Gothic cathedrals were being built, lime was the active ingredient in the mortar. Lime mortar isn't as strong as cement mortar, but it has more flexibility. Since cured lime mortar can be degraded by contact with water, many structures suffered from wind-blown rain over the centuries as water seeped through miniscule cracks. Survey your relationships for the seepage. Where are the cracks? From envy, resentfulness, betrayal, unresolved anger, misplaced priorities, unforgiveness, hurt, abandonment? Your family cathedral will weather, crack or even crumble without robust relationships.

*Dear Jonathan, Nicholas and Rachel,*

*Dads and moms don't always get it right. Sometimes we want so much to help, to support, to encourage our kids that it can be easily misunderstood as stifling and constraining. Ironically as we want the best for you, it can be misjudged as controlling, especially to a teen trying to find his own independence. That's exactly what happened between my dad and me. My dad (your Pop-Pop) was a stellar player on a dynasty football team – winning city championships year after year. I was a scrappy city kid who never played organized sports in his life; I learned to play in the parks of Philly in pick-up games with other neighborhoods. So when I made the football team and earned the honor to be captain at my suburban prep high school football team (La Salle College High School – Go Explorers!), I had already won the lottery. I loved the game, the unity and brotherhood of my team, and the mentoring of coaches that prepared us for games and life. We were having a terrible year. Dad had been increasingly frustrated with our poor performance and was very critical of coaches, players, me, the program – you name it. This went on every night for weeks making for tense car rides home from practice and dinner conversations. The cynicism and curt remarks just wore me down. Finally, I told my dad one night, "Please don't come to my games anymore." That Saturday morning, my mom drove me to my game in a very long and lonely trip. Midway through the first quarter I caught a glimpse of my dad hiding behind a tree watching the game. At first I was embarrassed to see my dad hiding from his son. But then I appreciated his defiant action which said what I longed to hear – "I want to see you play, not just see you win." When I got home he pretended not to already know we had won. When I gave him a hug, I whispered, "Maybe it's good luck when the fans stand behind the trees." My dad and I learned something valuable that changed our relationship. Remember to look for the wishes behind the words and intentions behind the misplaced remarks. Our relationship will be battle-tested by imperfect parenting, independent-minded children, bruised emotions, hurtful words, and misunderstood intentions. Meticulously work to untie the messy knots that inadvertently tangle up our relationships. You'll be glad you did. Love, Dad*

Storytelling connects family across generations. Not just names, but people with stories . . . cousins, great-grand parents, uncles and aunts, you. Cathedral building is about introducing family to their relatives, to their blood, to their spirit, to their character, to their imprinted beginnings, to those who carved their initials in your family cathedral.

## 2.7 Quarry Questions

1. *Write about annual traditions that began years ago.*

2. *Write story starters about those relationships that have meant the most to you – friends, teachers, coaches, moms and dads, brothers and sisters, grandparents, aunts and uncles.*

   *People who have sacrificed for you*
   *People who rescued you*
   *People who helped you see your gifts and potential*
   *People who pulled you out of the pit*
   *People who travelled with you to the peaks and valleys*
   *People who shaped your character, values, and steadfast beliefs*

*People who accepted you, believed in you, loved you with no strings attached*
*People who encouraged you to get up when you were down*
*People who took a chance on you and invested in you*
*People who provided a mirror when you needed it the most*

## 2.7 Legacy Letters

1. *Tell a story about one of the story starters above.*

2. *Write about a quote you heard or read that has inspired you.*

3. *Write about doing something you once thought you would never have the courage to do.*

4. *Write a letter of gratitude to a person above whose relationship influenced you even if that person is no longer living.*

# CHAPTER 3

# Building Your Legacy One Story at a Time

*Man is always a storyteller! He lives surrounded by his and others' myths. With them he sees everything in his life, no matter what befalls him. And he seeks to live his life as though he were telling it. —Sartre*

## The physics of writing your legacy

B efore we begin constructing our legacy, we need to understand the physics of writing stories that stick. Where do I start? Anywhere. What in the world do I write about? Content is easy. You have an incredible amount of material – a vast lifetime of wisdom, entertaining experiences, defining moments, epic adventures, unspoken gratitude. You don't need death-defying, larger-than-life stories to make an indelible mark on your family. Cathedrals aren't assembled with cast columns and prefab walls, but hand-chiseled stones that started as just pieces of rock. No particular stone is more meaningful or weighty than an adjacent one, but they are meticulously and methodically placed – stone by stone, in accord, conjoined – to form walls, columns, ceilings, cathedrals.

### Story writing needs Momentum

Legacy building requires a routine. Legacy building is deliberate, not transient work; it demands tenacity, not fleeting effort. In our busy lives, story writing to our family isn't natural, but we can establish a rhythm that generates momentum. Momentum emanates from the routine of inventorying shapeless story starters, disparate memories, unconnected experiences, then finding time later to chisel them into story stones. Social scientists and behaviorists have decoded how habits form. They require motivation, ability, a trigger, and a reward.

*Motivation.* To write your legacy, you need to be motivated. You need a rallying cause, an inspiration, a why. Why are you cathedral building your family legacy? What is it about legacy building that is important enough to give up your favorite television show or weekend football or get up early every Sunday or scribble a thought before going to sleep about how your daughter surprised you with her maturity? But your motivation can also include deadlines - wanting to influence your daughter before she starts her career; ensuring you are deeply connected to your son before teen identity woes; safeguarding your niece's heart before she starts dating; ensuring your grandson starts middle school with the fortitude to be himself even if his beliefs are a little awkward. Your motivation can also be socially steered. When we make a commitment to someone else, we tend to follow through. When others are participating in legacy writing, we tend to mutually hold each other accountable. Make a commit to friends, your spouse, your children and grandchildren, or other family members who want to legacy build with you – you will be more likely to follow-through.

*Ability.* Stones start in the quarry as amorphous pieces of rock, not intricately chiseled stones ready to be sealed with mortar. Start small. Make the first steps easy. You start legacy writing by digging in the quarry for story starters. Story starters are the raw ideas, the rough concepts, the memories, the uneven experiences, fractional phrases that you write about. Let your words be choppy, unpolished, and emotional. Set the bar low by deciding to write a story starter every day for one week. You are simply creating an inventory; you will chisel the choice stones, shape and polish them later. The environment matters when you legacy write – what lighting puts you at ease and inspires creativity, what seating makes you most comfortable, what type of pen and journal paper makes writing enjoyable?

Inspiration for your story starters doesn't need to be highly structured. Be playful. Rummage through boxes of photos and keepsakes. Your memories will flood back. When you take the time to reminisce, it will feel like the warmth of the sun on your face.

> *Finding Treasure.* Allocate some time to reviewing artifacts from the past. Find the poems you used to write or the diary entries. Take a rainy Sunday afternoon to peruse digital or physical photo albums, clean out your closet/attic/basement. Listen to music from eras in your life. What smells conjure memories? What food or meals do you remember? What sounds or music causes you to reminisce? Your thoughts will initially be random and seemingly jumbled. Have a notebook next to you. Salient memories will come into focus. Pay attention to the feelings that flood you. Notice how your pulse changes or how you start to tear up or why you shake your head. Some stories will leave a smile on your face, joy in your heart and others may drum anger, regret and resentment. Avoid the tendency to filter or evaluate them. Pay attention to the words you say or think to yourself . . . They are distinctive marks for your story starters.
>
> *I can't believe I used to . . .*
> *I remember that vacation, I was having a really hard year in school and Dad was so thoughtful . . .*
> *I can't imagine what I was thinking going out with him . . .*

*I can't believe I made it through that period of my life . . .*
*Whenever I hear that song, I think to myself . . .*

*Capture your everyday and not-so-everyday moments.* We are writing new stories every day. Find a way to capture the everyday moments immediately before you lose the emotions and the meaning - make a voice memo on your phone, write a little note to yourself, journal at the beginning/end of the day. Your mindfulness and consciousness of your everyday moments will enrich your writing and allow you to appreciate how legacy is being written every day. I have clunky phrases and fragmented sentences keyed into *Evernote*, a note taking app on my mobile. I have dozens of sticky notes, index cards, napkins with scribbled notes. Look for the pattern and connections between them.

> *Waking up on the first morning of our canoe trip in Canada with my arm around Jonathan and a cup of steaming coffee watching the sun rise over the trees. Still. Loons cackling. The air so fresh it seemed to cleanse our lungs with every breath. He anxiously anticipated a day of paddling, portaging, exploring. Two years later Nick and I would journey the same trip – finding an unmarked island to ourselves we named Buckles Island. (date)*

> *Jonathan excited he won writing competition for his grade. Wrote about our canoeing trip to Canada – didn't realize it was such a mile marker for him. He sent a thank-you note to his former middle school English teacher for preparing him to write so well. Proud of how he handles "wins" with humility and gratitude. (date)*

> *Rachel and I role playing* Sleeping Beauty. *Take after take until I got it right. A delicate kiss on the cheek (not forehead)*

*with a flower in my hand (not a tulip, but a rose). Filled her heart. I cherished being her Prince Charming and worked hard to set the bar high ☺ (date)*

*Cooked great seafood gumbo with Nicholas. He loves to cook. He dreams when cooking – opens something inside him – creativity, enjoyment. Connects us. Conversation about what's really happening in his heart flows easily. (date)*

*Playing Disney Monopoly today with Rachel. We placed a wager – whoever wins gets a cookie. "Game on," said Rachel. But as we prepared the board for play, she said, "Dad, what if you lose. I'll feel bad getting a cookie without you." I leaned over and whispered into her ear. "Playing with you makes me feel like I've already won." She gave me an endearing look and said, "I love you, Daddy." (date)*

*Jonathan was having a crabby start to his day and Rachel abruptly said, "Jonathan, are you being God-centered or self-centered today?" Throw-down from little seven-year-old Rachel to her eighth-grade big brother. I wasn't having the best day that day either until Rachel's words reminded me to focus on the right things. (date)*

*One of his friends started picking on a new girl at school. Nick defended her, said something inside him made him blurted out, "Hey, that's not very nice. Would you say that about me?" "That's different," his friend said. "No it's not." Nick remembered what it's like to be on the outside, teased and tormented by careless words that make you not feel good enough. He's on the other side now – popular and well liked. He could have turned the cheek. I'm so proud of him…He is too. He learned something about himself today. (date)*

*Be whimsical.* Storytell about the nuances that make you smirk, the family customs that are amusing, the eccentric behaviors that are playful memories, the quirky stories that cause you to burst out laughing.

Recount those morning routines – strategies to get your kids up and ready for the day, favorite breakfasts, weekend traditions.

Recount those evening routines with your family – study habits of your kids, homework bane and glory, and goodnight and tuck-in moments.

Recall conversations – on the porch, lying in bed with your kids, around the fireplace, family meetings; walking in the door from work when your kids would spill their day to you. The conversations about love, about the birds and bees, about getting engaged, about choosing your first job.

Remember the stories behind their pet names and nicknames.

Remember your first weekend away from parents or first time living on your own.

Recollect family parties and holidays – funny moments, laugh-until-you-cry pranks, odd foods, special recipes, contentious games, and spirited debates.

Reminisce about favorite vacations and summer adventures – places where time seemed to stop, family hobbies and pastimes, experiences that knitted your family together.

Pause and reflect on your inventory occasionally. Don't rush. Each time you look at it, you will find something that calls you to write or deepen your understanding. Then choose a rock from your inventory and chisel it into a story stone. It seems that about 300 to 500 words is about maximum for simple stories to have punch. Just start writing then go back and trim the extraneous. You can write however you wish, but there seems to be a repeatable pattern legacy writers use:

1.  set up / situation
2.  what happened / twist / tension
3.  address family via application / lesson learned
4.  affirm and encourage family

Share stories with family and use some of their story themes as inspiration. You will inevitably quarry even more story starters – similar stories, different contexts; never-thought-to-write-about-that ideas. You will discover clever approaches to chisel your stones – how to delicately talk about certain topics, how to navigate sensitivities, how to write in a colloquial voice.

When the message is clear, compelling, and simple, it's worth repeating. We need to be masters of exclusion by focusing on singular messages. Save back stories, sub-plots, and character development sidebars for additional stories – don't be afraid to break one story into two. It's better to tell multiple stories and have them woven together as threads than a ball of yarn that can easily be tangled into a mess with a mistakenly implied message. Are you writing about your first car to explain the thrill of working so hard to earn it, the exhilarating freedom of getting away from home, or surviving a devastating car crash in it? Don't squeeze both in the same story.

*Determine the Trigger.* You need a trigger, a reminder for legacy writing. Find the margin to write. What time and place allows you to think freely while also establishing a repetitive routine? Routine is vital, so start with a definitive goal (e.g., writing one story starter every

Saturday and Sunday morning with a cup of coffee and a biscotti). You need to put it on your calendar, set a reminder on your phone, write it on your refrigerator, or substitute it with another routine like watching a television show every Thursday night. When can you decompress and reflect? Is there a day of the week or a time of day that you can commit to? Maybe you designate Sunday after dinner as a time for you to reflect on your week and write some stories. Maybe you quarry some story stones by getting up fifteen minutes early every other day or just Saturdays. Maybe you write on weekend afternoons while your spouse watches sports or shops. Set a time and a place and stick to the routine.

*Reward yourself.* The adherence to a routine is important for habit formation, but you also need a reward. After months of tiresome stone carving and placement, cathedral builders could see the silhouette of a column or the walls shadow the sunlight. With gladness and satisfaction they relished in the tangible progress. Share your stories with your family. Drop them in an envelope and mail it to them whether you are traveling internationally or living at the same address. You may do it frequently or just on special occasions like birthdays. Maybe you share a story with beloved family every Mother's Day or Father's Day, Christmas or Thanksgiving. Start a tradition for family to bring a story to share and listen around the kitchen table at holiday gatherings. Let the words seep into the room and fill it up with wisdom and love. Over time, you will notice certain behaviors fade away or switch on. Your reward will be noticing your son or daughter's choices as more considerate, careful, and deliberate. You may notice a tiny bit of coy affection or a gentle request for your counsel. You may not notice a dramatic reaction immediately, but know that you have imprinted something meaningful into their lives.

---

"Genuine influence goes deeper than getting people to do what you want them to do. It means people pick up where you left off because they believe." — The Story Factor

---

Let the momentum of your story writing capture the aliveness of your life with a vantage point that is both panoramic and telescopic. Your history is made up of unadorned legacy-generating experiences being created every day. The busyness of life can be a veil to the simple events in your family that matter immensely in filling the vessels of our family drop by drop, imprinting their hearts, curing the mortar. Watch and listen intently. Slow down and remind yourself to appreciate the bubble baths, gingerbread houses, homeless blanket collection, strenuous hikes and lazy-day fishing, bedtime stories and late-night homework help, bike rides, school plays and team tryouts, homecoming from college, cocoa on chilly mornings, box forts and game nights on weekends. These stories nourish us; they provide the kind of food our soul craves.

### Story writing needs Magnetism

Sticky stories pull; they don't push. They have magnetism that connects the storyteller with the listener. And you need to connect before you can convince. Facts about family circumstances are inert. Stories have life. Stories engender faith. And faith is what allows people to believe in you and overcome their obstacles, achieve their goals, power through their pain. Before they trust your wisdom, they need to know you. Before your family will allow themselves to be influenced by your story, they need to have faith in you. And faith needs a story to propel it.

You are more than a storyteller – you are family. Let your stories expose your humanity – triumphs and failures, tears of joy and anguish. Let your stories open windows to the depths of your life not in one sweeping epic, but through a series of stories that bares a rousing journey. We all have a desire to be known. Not superficially, but completely. How do I want to be remembered? Am I really known? Do your children know how hard you work at your marriage? Do they see your integrity at work? Do they know that you spend countless hours mentoring and developing those who may ultimately lead you? Do they know what social causes you fight for? Do they know why you sacrifice financially, yet give generously – why two jobs, why you pack a lunch, why you don't eat seconds and give them the extras on their plates? Do they understand your past struggles with envy and your secret for overcoming it? Do they know your prayers for them . . . for weeks, years, decades?

*Dear Jonathan, Nicholas, and Rachel,*

*When I was in fourth grade, I had a speech impediment. I could not pronounce words correctly having an "S" or an "R." Now, there are lots of words in the dictionary using those letters, so you can imagine how frustratingly difficult speaking was for me. When I'd read aloud, I just couldn't make the sounds come out of my mouth fittingly – "R" would come out like "W" and "S" would come out like "TH." Kids laughed at me . . . You know how mean some can be. Several times a week, I was excused from class and marshalled to a speech therapist. Progress was slow. Then I avoided speaking altogether and I became self-conscious, shy and withdrawn. When public speaking in front of my class was required for reports, I'd be sleepless for a week. Then in fifth grade I had a teacher, Sister Paul Joseph. She was actually more than a teacher; she was my encourager. She invited me one day to participate in a public speaking contest. I avoided any direct conversations with her for weeks as the deadline for signing up quickly approached. But then she told me how she specifically asked me to represent our school. I reluctantly agreed. I chose a speech by Napoleon, a farewell to his troops – it had the fewest number of R's and S's. We practiced three times a week for several months. Enunciating, gesturing, pausing, pacing. I prayed something; anything would happen so that I wouldn't have to give that speech. I'll never forget the knotted stomach giving my speech to an audience of parents and evaluators. My dad didn't want to make me more nervous so he had his head down through my entire speech. When I sat back down next to him, his eyes swelled with tears, he whispered to me, "Son, I didn't even know that was you. Your booming voice . . . your speech, your words were perfect. I'm so proud of you." Though I didn't win the contest, I won a battle inside of me that day that has carried me through the years. Sister Paul Joseph nudged me to courageously dispel a self-limiting, twisted lie I was telling myself – "not good enough." Find those moments in your life when you feel incapable or incompetent and challenge yourself to overcome your fear. Like my teacher was to me, be a person that encourages others by giving them a chance to overcome something or uncover something deep inside themselves. Don't miss those defining moments in your life that can spark something anew in you. Love, Dad.*

Families are naturally inquisitive about their history, but legacy building is more than who we are related to. Our genealogy is a step toward a much deeper connection to our family, but dotted lines linking unfamiliar names can't write their legacy. Besides, genealogy exercises with family invariably begins or ends with "what were they like?" questions. If you want to get to know someone, you need to get to know their story. It wasn't until my grandfather's funeral with military carrying his American flag-draped casket that I grasped the honor of his military service in World War I. His distant stares and startled bursts from afternoon naps came into grasp. Kids are naturally curious about their grandparents and great-grandparents, aunts and uncles, distant cousins. They want to know more than just the ancestry; they want to know the stories.

*Dear Sara & Andrew:*

*Did I ever tell you how my dad had such a tremendous impact on my work ethic and work-life balance? Grandpa was high school-educated and, grew up only knowing his mother, as his own dad died when he was two. Life wasn't easy in the 1920's and Grandpa spent much of his childhood having very little of life's simple pleasures, that we now take for granted. Later, he and Grandma raised six kids in the 1960's – another very challenging time – and without a college education, Grandpa worked a lot of menial jobs, from driving an oil truck, to working the county fairgrounds, to custodial work at the local school. He worked long, hard hours at jobs that provided little satisfaction or opportunity for advancement. Yet, he was there every night at the dinner table and was always interested in our day. He struck a great balance between his work life and his home life, and while I know he must have had more than his share of terribly frustrating days, he left it at the door before he walked in each night.*

*So why am I telling you this now, after you have left home and are starting lives on your own? Because I pray you will always strike a good balance between your careers and the families you will create someday. I know that I struggled with this, throughout my career, where work consumed my days and multi-night travel was common. But, like Grandpa, I always tried to be present to you when I was home, and left my work challenges at the door. It was important to keep our home and family life stable, which would allow you to better adjust to the day-to-day challenges you faced growing up. That is the reason why I never accepted a role that would cause us to uproot from our home and relocate to another city, as I believed that no matter how demanding things got at work, if I could maintain a foundation of stability at home – you would be better for it. It was a choice I will never regret.*

*And so now that you are at the starting line of your career, armed with a strong work ethic, but before you have families of your own – make a commitment to God that you will always strive to seek that balance between your career and your family. Love, Dad*

Legacy demands listening to our own story. Every great story has a plot. When you survey your life, what plot does your story have? What themes emerge? What does the top of the jigsaw puzzle box look like? It's tempting to role play "might have been" stories or retell others' stories because they seem more captivating. It's tempting to sugarcoat, to gloss-over, to exaggerate, to force fit, to wear masks and hide behind fake stories. But let the beauty of your story unfold through your authenticity. Let *you* emerge, not some false persona of a person you wish you would have become. What do you want them to know about you? How do you want them to know you? They wonder, *what was Mom like before she was a mom? What were you like as a kid? What was it like growing up? What did you learn along the way? What does Dad do when someone isn't looking? What is Mom like at work to people who gossip about her? How does Mom take care of the people that work for her? I know I get punished for things I do wrong, but you, Dad? Dad, were you ever a bully? Mom, did a boy ever make you cry? Dad, do you ever cry? Mom, did someone ever break your heart?*

*Dear Jonathan, Nicholas, and Rachel,*

*Save and sacrifice for something you want. I was desperately saving for graduate school. Tuition was expensive; Mom and I decided we didn't want to borrow from our future with debt. I was working 40 hours a week in my engineering job at Kimberly-Clark and also working at Sueann's Bagels several days a week from 2:30 a.m. to 7:30 a.m. baking bagels. (Because your dad is color blind there were a lot of accidently burnt blueberry bagels that year.) Over several months I visited MBA programs and interviewed to be admitted. One weekend, I pulled into Nashville to visit Vanderbilt and was smitten with its Southern flair. I saw a pair of cowboy boots that I loved. They weren't the most expensive boots on the rack, but they were more than I could afford . . . unless avoided a similar costing item— my hotel room. So I purchased the cowboy boots and drove around the Vanderbilt campus looking for a place to park my car and hunker down for the night. It was a miserable night. Sleeping in the backseat of my car was incredibly uncomfortable and I'd never recommend it unless you really had to. I didn't have to, but I wanted to . . . for a pair of really cool cowboy boots. I still have those cowboy boots and I love them. Shoes, clothing aren't that important to me, but those boots bring a smile to my face every time I wear them. I have had dozens of shoes in my life – none have really mattered to me except those boots. There is something about saving for something you love that makes you appreciate it; there's something about the story behind your sacrifice – the emotion, the intention, the heavy-going, the elated enjoyment – that makes it so much more enjoyable and appreciated. Save and sacrifice for something you want. Love, Dad*

## 3.1 Quarry Questions

1. *When are you at your best? Ask at least five people to write a short example when you have been at your best. Ask co-workers, spouse, moms and dads, brothers and sisters, grandparents, aunts and uncles, cousins, your volunteer community organizations, friends and neighbors. The results will encourage you and may even surprise you. Sometimes others see something in us that we just can't. Write down the phrases from each letter. Can you see a pattern revealed?*

2. *What authentic stories about you does your family need to hear? What stories pierce the façade and expose another hidden side of you?*

3. *Write down the poignant stories that come to mind during life-stages: toddler, young child, elementary, middle and high school years, post high school/early career, engagement, newlywed, pregnancy, parenting, empty nesting, grand parenting, retiring.*

4. *Take excerpts of old performance reviews and put them into story starters. What do your peers and boss say about you?*

5. *What are your "up all night" stories?*

6. *Make a list of story starters to request your family to bring letters at the next gathering. Examples: what was the best present you ever received? What was great advice passed down to you and when did using it make a difference?*


## 3.1 Legacy Letters

1. *Tell us a story of when you were at your best using the story starters in (1) above.*

2. *Tell personal stories about the "why" behind:*

   *Defining moments: transformational moments, a-ha moments, growth through trial*

   *Favorites: adventures, vacations, places to visit, books and movies, hymns and songs, holidays*

   *Firsts: first paycheck, first date, first ticket, first time you felt proud, first time feeling different, first apartment, first home, first time away from home, first time on your own*

   *Relationships: how you met your husband/wife, when you decided to get engaged, wedding day memories; poor/great relationship decisions*

   *Parenting: favorite memories of your kids as they grew through different life stages; advice passed down from your parents; why is parenting the job of a lifetime, a calling, a privilege?*

   *Working: first job, types of jobs, best job and worst job, best boss/worst boss, what would people always say about you, why people loved to work with you, how you start/finish your day, wisdom on work-family balance, bright moments and dark moments*

*Spirituality: what and why do you believe; how do you live out your spirituality? Why is your faith so fervent?*

### Story writing needs Energy

An object can store energy due to its change in position – its potential energy. When you draw a bow or a spring, the change from its usual position stores energy available for work. When you remove the external force holding the spring, it converts the stored potential energy to the kinetic energy of motion.

The potential energy of your stories is amplified when you introduce emotion. Common sense stories are expected and they aren't very sticky. It's not that they don't have a role. But if you want lessons to be remembered, then you need a message that is sticky and sticky messages are emotional and unexpected. When your audience feels through your stories, their position changes; they need a moment; they let out a gasp, a wow, an oh, a sigh, a chuckle; they have butterflies, welling eyes, a big smile, an ascending pulse. Emotion pulls the string back creating a tension – the potential to activate maybe not immediately, but at an impending moment. Emotion pulls rather than pushes. Feelings move people. Your story is ripe with emotion, you just need to tap it.

---

"I've learned that people will forget what you said, people will forget what you did, but people will never forget how you made them feel." — Maya Angelou

---

Often when people storytell, they hold back because they don't want to look corny or weak, self-aggrandizing or boastful, sentimental or foolish. But playing it safe doesn't unlock an emotional connection with your audience. Don't let your desire to appear sensible, profound, or witty keep you from displaying your humanness and touching others. When our potential energy emanates from ego – what others think of us – our stories are inert, static, flat. When our potential energy arises from emotion, it opens others' hearts and our stories can trigger; they can motivate; they can be a kinetic force for change. If you want to get their attention, if you want your message to linger with them for a while, if you want your message to be recalled at just the right moment, then you need them to feel your story.

*Dear Jonathan, Nicholas, and Rachel,*

*I had a teacher in high school who was a wonderful man named Brother Linus. Brother Linus was a Christian Brother teacher at LaSalle College High School. On the first day of class, he had us all sit in alphabetical order. We were assigned a number. Brother Linus never called us by our first name, but rather would call out "Number 15 boy" or "Number 3 boy." It seemed so impersonal to me . . . Everyone was just a number to him. But Brother Linus loved being a role model for impressionable teen boys. We'd hang out with him after school. What was remarkable about Brother Linus was his dedicated hobby at night. He would call dozens of "his boys" (current students and alums) on their birthday. "Hello, can I speak with Number 27 boy?" The first time it happened, my mom answered the phone and stood there with a blank look on her face. "You have the wrong number." He repeated it. "There's a strange man on the phone asking for Number 27 boy." I grabbed the phone from her. "Today is a special day, Number 27 boy. Happy Birthday. You are special and God made only one of you." Brother Linus would spend a few minutes chatting with each of his students every year on their birthday. Even when I went to college, Brother Linus called my home and then he called me at the University of Wisconsin.*

*My roommate had the same blank expression when he called my dorm room. "Uh, someone is calling here asking for Number 27." How special I felt on some lonely birthdays far from home to get a call from a dear teacher who personally made my birthday a celebration every year. One year, I didn't get the call from Brother Linus. That was the birthday that I cried because I knew my elderly teacher was gone. You never know how even the little things – a phone call from a kindhearted teacher – can be so comforting and uplifting to lonely boys homesick. In a world that reinforces satisfying our own needs, I hope you don't forget the power of touching others and intersecting with their lives. Culture will have you believe that those intersections are interruptions in pursuit of your own goals and needs, but I tell you that they are so fulfilling and worth pushing the pause button in life. Be selfless in sharing – not just what you physically have, but from your essence – words of encouragement and assurance and faith, small acts of kindness and gratitude and mentoring. You never know when you'll be encouraging someone else's mommy or daddy like Brother Linus encouraged your daddy. Love, Dad*

You can't make someone listen to you. You need to entice and inspire them; you need to fascinate and transfix them. Your story needs to come alive. Emotions are behind every story and every decision in your life, so get emotional. Tell stories with your voice – your tone, your pauses and emphasis, your unrefined language, your virtual inflections, your implicit moments of silence, your calm whisper, your crackled voice. Let them feel your warmth, your embrace, your hug.

*It took me two years to write this letter. I didn't think I was even strong enough to finish it, but then I thought of leaving this as a treasured gift for you . . .*

*I was crushed under the weight of this decision...I couldn't escape. I was distracted by it waking up, showering, driving to work, in meetings, at meals. I was torturing myself by recalling how a few simple, honest statements could have avoided all of this . . .*

*When I staggered off the airplane, seeing her with open arms and a big, bright smile, a flood of emotion just swelled inside me and I burst into tears. I-I-I had endlessly rehearsed what to say for weeks. "I'm sorry. I'm sorry for the cruel words that hurt you and . . ." but I just choked on the words and I let my long embrace finish my plea for forgiveness. That started our healing process for the next six years . . .*

*When the doctor came into the room, his somber look said it all. Months of ebullient hope seemed to evaporate from Dad. This man who has been my knight-in-shining armor for more than twelve years was crushed and defeated. I looked him right in the eyes, squeezed his hand, and said with searing confidence, "We will beat this."*

Words come from our wounds. Words come from our mountaintops. Words come from our heart. After all what's behind your story is not hollow characters or objects; there are people behind your stories. Not just people, your family. Take your family by the hand on a brief emotional journey.

*Victoria, Jacob Thomas, Matthew, Mark William, Lucas, and Zachary,*

*One day when I was in eighth grade, I went to school like any other day. But, I was pulled from my classroom and asked to go down to the principal's office. I found out that my dad had had an accident. He had been pulled off of the roof of a building and was badly injured. I remember being in the elevator at the hospital with him while he was helpless and bloody being wheeled between procedures. It was strange to see my dad in such a weakened, injured, and fragile state. He had a broken jaw, a shattered wrist, a broken elbow, his pager had been driven into his side, etc. The wrist was so bad that he had an external fixture drilled through his skin into the bone to keep the bones in place until they healed. I had no idea at that time that he would be alright. He was badly injured but could easily have been killed by a twenty-foot plummet down to asphalt.*

*My dad was always a hard worker, whether at work or at home. He left for work early in the morning, came home for dinner sometimes late, and was often on call for emergency refrigeration service. That summer, Dad was off of work, at home recovering from his wounds. That was an unusual summer. I have a particularly vivid memory of that summer, even the songs on the radio. Later my sister Julie told my dad that summer was the best one of her life. Why could such a tragic accident and injuries make for a good summer? It was because Dad was at home. Children, spend time together as a family – savory and enjoy it as a priceless luxury and gift. Love, Daddy*

## 3.2 Quarry Questions

1. *Make two columns – one for positive feelings and one for negative feelings – for the most frequent feelings in your life. Here are some to consider: tender, affectionate, finally free, surprised, adored, uncomfortable, humbled, joyful, special, embarrassed, lost, lonely, deeply distraught, boldly brave.*

2. *Make rows of the various lifestages – youngster, teen, young adult, early career, newly married/committed, new parent, mid-career, etc. Write the top three emotions for each life-stage.*

3. *Write down in your Legacy Letter journal some emotionally charged (positive or negative) events in your life.*

4. *What emotions are easy for you to reveal and which are more difficult?*

*3.2 Legacy Letters*

1. *Choose one of the feelings from above then tell a story. Don't play it safe. Let your emotions flow.*

2. *Choose one of the emotionally charged events in your life in (3) above and write a story.*

### The Five P's of Sticky Storytelling

We want to write stories that are sticky. That stay with us like our first love. That complete us like an old friend. That warm us on the inside like looking through photo albums. That cause our heart to race when we turn to that letter. Sticky stories are compelling. They break our paradigms, alter our tightly held beliefs, reframe our conventions, and capture attention enough for our family to follow our lead despite not knowing exactly where you are taking them. Sticky stories are memorable. They stay with us, easily recalled when staring at a decision, and survive in our family because they are unexpected. Sticky stories are repeatable. They are simple enough to be told not just once, but picked up and recited from generation to generation.

#### *Storytelling on Purpose*

*What is your why?* Your stories need to have purpose, resolve, determination. Stories aren't like striking up a conversation without knowing where it may go. We can't write stories like we call up mom/dad, siblings, or kids on Sunday afternoon to catch-up. Some stories seem to be pushed on us. Finger pointing to embarrass others, back-biting to save face, dragging others' reputation to reap revenge. While they may be interesting, they are not embedding because their story *why* is fleeting. Good stories, the stories that are read over and over again, don't need finger pointing or artificial drama to captivate their audiences. Your stories need to pull so that family with their own free will come close to you and listen for your wisdom from a spirit of trustworthiness. Before you start writing, contemplate, *what is my purpose?* What do I want to convey to my son or daughter, grandson or granddaughter, niece or nephew? What do you want to imprint in them in this story? What do I want them to remember and recall? Listen to your heart, not just your head. Why does your story need to be told?

---

"You will find as you look back upon your life that the moments when you have really lived are the moments when you have done things in the spirit of love." — Henry Drummond (Poet)

---

*Enlighten them.* Like the Doppler Effect, we hear a train coming with a crescendo signal - we see the story unfolding, the plot thickening, the characters developing. We know what's coming because it's all too familiar but for your family it's all new. Life requires choices and you have the hindsight to give the gift of foresight to your family. Your stories can provide them with the instincts to anticipate, to prepare, to hear the familiar sounds coming right at them. Why allow them to experience avoidable pain when life has enough unavoidable hurt and aching and stinging? Let your trailblazing expose the headshaking consequences and hindsight relief of choosing certain paths. Let them see fulfillment from generosity, the boomerang benefits from serving others, the buoyance from faith.

Write your life lessons for them full of wisdom and insight like family parables. Pass down treasured lessons from their ancestors that capture their spirit, remember their sacrifice, honor their values. What elements of the past do you not want repeated for your family? Flash up "Yield" or "Caution" signs. How will life leave them thirsty if they aren't careful? How are they likely to be trapped – dead-end roads, a little lost, a little scared? How can you punctuate the significance of your family values?

*Dear Jonathan, Nicholas and Rachel,*

*Share. It's easier when you don't have much. But you will find that the more you have, the less you want to give. It's easy to declare your generosity in the future, but you really need a personal commitment that springs from your heart – Give. Give of your time. Share the talents you have for the sake of others. Give of your money. Share your wealth with those that need it. Give with no-strings-attached. I have been most joyful, content, peaceful, alive when I have given. You never know what hangs in the balance of giving to someone else – you may be just what they need at the time. Whether it's providing money to orphans in impoverished countries or helping to fundraise for second-chance homes for teen moms or listening to a friend who is struggling. I was flying back from a business trip early in my career. I was upgraded to first class. I had a particularly long day and hadn't eaten anything in more than eight hours. I was excited to relax and get a little food and something to drink. As I was sitting at the gate, a soldier sat next to me. We started a conversation and I learned that he was coming home from the Gulf War, just a flight away from seeing his family. I asked him if he wanted to sit in first class. At first he declined, but I insisted as someone who valued his service to our country. His face looked as if he hit the jackpot. On the flight I was close enough to peer at his enjoyment of the hot meal and cold beer. He was so thankful coming off the flight and introduced me to his family who was waiting for their son and brother to be home. Giving will not likely earn you a reputation of power, but something more valuable – a generous person. Love, Dad*

*Enrich them.* You know them – what do they need? Sometimes we don't need to be more careful with our words; we need to be more explicit with our words. It's often the things not said that can be as hurtful as the things said. Words unspoken still say something.

Silence signals apathy and ambivalence. Apathy and ambivalence in families shouts, "I don't care." Enrich them with words of affirmation and let them know they matter. They will live up to the expectations they hear from you. Affirm her inner beauty and outer elegance, the heartfulness and graciousness of your sweet daughter, granddaughter, or niece. Affirm his strength and courage and charisma. Tell him how you gush with pride when you tell neighbors about the man he is at work and husband he is at home. Impress their worthiness – how precious a gift they are to you, how much you cherish them, treasure shared memories, and admire the men and women they are.

Our stories should notice – notice their small steps toward maturity; notice the little things that can easily get lost in a hurried day; notice not just the A's, but the effort; notice their kindness; notice how good you feel walking in the door and seeing them; notice their intonations, nuances, mannerisms. Noticing allows you to course correct drifting. Noticing speaks volumes about how much you care. It's a lifelong need – to be noticed by mom and dad, to be worthy of their unconditional love. In a life of priorities, they need to see themselves at the front of the line.

*Dear Jonathan, Nicholas and Rachel,*

*I hope you have the amazing privilege of a family. If you do, you'll never regret putting your family first. One thing is certain: You are easily replaceable at work (sobering, but true), but you are never replaceable at home. In a world of measuring and rewarding progress, how can you measure progress at home? At work, you can count progress. You win awards. You accomplish tasks and receive praise. You can easily get caught up in the applause of others; it can be intoxicating. At home, in the vacancy of counting success, in the dim of applause, you can be deceived that your presence doesn't matter. But you will always be missed at home. After a team dinner for an important project at work, everyone was going out to celebrate at a bar around the corner. Sounds like college years calling back – pool table, dart board, live band. After a week of rigor, it was incredibly inviting. I liked my team and knew the professional importance of socially connecting with people. I just had one very significant request holding me back – Jonathan's algebra homework. He had been calling me throughout the dinner meeting that evening asking me for help and I promised "to be home by 8:30." I could lie and say the decision was easy; it wasn't. I really wanted to go out and have a good time especially after a grinding week of hard work. But being a parent requires a commitment to those we love especially when they need us the most. By returning home, I made a decision that I would make hundreds if not thousands of times as a father – I chose my family first. I remember Jonathan giving me a big hug and thanking me for coming home. That was applause enough for me. Love, Dad.*

We need to look back occasionally to see progress, to see the growth spurts – you're not the man or woman you used to be and neither are your children. We can't see the progress without looking for the outcomes. Razor-thin, scheduled lives disallows for time to pause and take in the man he is becoming. Notice how he doesn't interrupt his girlfriend when she is speaking but his friends do. Notice how she handled the harsh words of her employee. Create the margin in your busy life to see their development.

*Encourage them.* Encourage them to be gritty and preserve through hardships. Encourage them to be curious and pioneering. Encourage them to be steadfast in their values and moral choices when culture seems to gravitationally pull them off course. Encourage them to share their gifts and give to those who need help. Encourage them with the sureness that you will stand with them in the trials of life. Encourage them to flee or stand tall. Encourage them that mistakes aren't endings, setbacks aren't death sentences. Encourage them to trust and find God when they feel elated in triumphs or empty in despair.

In <u>Wisdom of our Fathers</u>, famous newscaster Tim Russert depicts powerful stories of relationships between children and their fathers. He shares a personal story about his son, Luke, that underscores the process and reward of encouraging, accepting, and unconditionally loving your family.

*"The graduating seniors received their yearbooks that day, and each student had been given a full page to reflect on his high school career. That night, when I got to bed, I began flipping through Luke's copy. His page began with expressions of gratitude. 'Dad,' said the first one, 'you're the driving force behind it all, and my best friend in the world. Thanks for always having my back. I love you.'*

*"Now if you had asked me to identify a specific moment when I had Luke's back, I couldn't point to one. He was reminding me that tender moments are the ultimate wisdom – whether it's the mutual love and respect that two parents share, a supportive word, or one of the many little comments and gestures of daily life that are more powerful than any lecture. Small moments accumulate and last a lifetime and, what's more, they get carried into the next generation. I lay back, smiled, and closed my misty eyes. The pillow never seemed so soft."*

*3.3 Quarry Questions*

1. *What words of encouragement do you anticipate your family needing most in their life journey? In their relationships, how they manage money, what they do with their spare time?*

2. *Spend some time this week noticing your family. What strikes you that you overlooked before? Can you see their clear paths or how they might be drifting? How can you enrich them right now?*

3. *For each of your children/grandchildren, make a list of life lessons that you know they will need in their life because you can "hear the train coming" like the Doppler Effect in life.*

*3.3 Legacy Letters*

1. *Write a story exemplifying a life lesson your family will need in (3) above.*

2. *Write a story that notices something remarkable in each of your children/grandchildren.*

---

"Many people suppressed their feelings in order to keep peace with others. We cannot control the reactions of others. However, although people may initially react when you change the way you are by speaking honestly, in the end it raises the relationship to a whole new and healthier level. Either that or it releases the unhealthy relationship from your life. Either way, you win." — Bronnie Ware, The Five Regrets of the Dying

---

### Storytelling with a Pure Heart

Authentically telling your story requires bravery and vulnerability. Candidly transferring life's hard lessons requires nerve. When we write stories, we have a proclivity to put ourselves in the best light or conceal some of the darkness. Are you prepared to write with authenticity and genuineness? Are you prepared to chisel away at your pride, at your ego, at your self-sufficiency, at your pretenses? To remove the façades and reveal your realness? Preaching that patience is a virtue is a waste unless you are willing to expose the bitter consequences of impatience or the far-reaching pleasure of seeing your patience unfold to strengthen a strained relationship. Storytelling with a pure heart chips away at the wall we build to protect ourselves. But paradoxically, it's in your authenticity that you are strongest for your family.

To pull your audience, your stories need a pure heart. This means you write with your heart in the right place, a heart focused on building a multigenerational legacy and not your reputation. Hindsight isn't 20/20 if your heart is distorted. A tainted heart embellishes and perverts the truth. Façades falsify the realness of the events and emotions. Masking the realness – the clumsiness, the consequences, the embarrassment, the devastation, the despair, the falsehoods – fails to transfer your intended lesson. Preserving your ideal characterizations are veneers in your cathedral that aren't likely to be enduring. A drop of insincerity or falsehood or inauthenticity will sour your stories; fissure your foundation; close the door to your vestibule. Shoddy stones and construction techniques eventually get exposed over time causing your family to dismiss not just a single story, but perhaps all of your stories. And then entire walls collapse in your cathedral.

When our heart is pure then our wisdom can be clear. Having a pure heart means owning your past – taking accountability for decisions and conceding the consequences. We most certainly cannot speak prudence venerably to our family when skeletons are hiding in the closet; when our character is in doubt; when our covert past is whispered among family. Secrets seep and break hearts. It isn't an unblemished past that our family craves. When we ignore the past, we carry the weight of those decisions into the future including imprinting poor decision to our family. When we dismiss abandoning our family by hiding behind shallow explanations, we not only fail to prevent it from occurring again, but also fail to imprint its dreadfulness to your family. Let them implicitly experience life lessons through you so they can avoid the abyss themselves. Teach them lessons from your past to avoid repeating them in their future. Let them implicitly experience the triumphant lessons that you wish repeated over and over again.

*Dear Cole, Peyton, and Walker,*

*When I was growing up, my brother struggled with alcohol and drugs. In fact, alcoholism was a problem with various members of our family. Some used it as an escape from relationships that seemed difficult to deal with, others with stresses at work to fill the void of loneliness. The choices family members made didn't just affect them. Their choices affected everyone around them causing a lot of hurt and pain to others.*

*I dealt with the pain my family was going through as my brother struggled with his addictions by focusing on my grades and getting involved in lots of activities – plays, student council, sports, etc. I guess I thought that if I was a "model child" it would take some negative attention away from my brother. What this habit did, however, was lead me to believe that my value and worth was based on performance. I had to achieve to be of value. On the surface, this seems like a secret to success – I got good grades, went to a good college, got a good job, made a lot of money, etc. However, it was exhausting and unsatisfying. To feel valued, I needed to do more, accomplish more. This mentality also put a strain on my relationships. Instead of unconditionally loving the people in my life who meant the most to me, I was unnecessarily critical and got resentful if they weren't doing as much as I was.*

*As I have grown through life, I have enjoyed the peace of realizing that there is nothing I can do or anyone can do to demonstrate their value. No amount of awards, no salary level or job title, no amount of volunteer hours, no achievement makes you a better person, defines you, validates you. You are fearfully, beautifully and wonderfully made (Psalm 139:14) – as you are. Perhaps it was when I became your mom that I started to get this. There is nothing you need to do to prove to me that I should love you and be proud of you. I already love you with an indescribable intensity and I am so proud of you – even when you stumble or make a mistake. What's amazing is that God loves you and is proud of you with an intensity that goes way beyond what I am capable of. When you were little, I used to tuck you in and whisper to you, "You are strong and smart and very kind. I am so proud of you and I will always love you, no matter what!" These words hold true today and forever. Love, Mom*

Is your heart pure to narrate? Without blinders. Without the twisted tales and stretched truth. Raw. Unpolished. In her book <u>Daring Greatly</u>, Brene Brown tells us, "vulnerability is the core, the heart, the center, of meaningful human experiences . . . Vulnerability is about sharing our feelings and our experiences with people who have earned the right to hear them. Being vulnerable and open is mutual and an integral part of the trust-building process." Be real. Engage with your family from a place of vulnerability. Vulnerability is the precursor to authenticity. Vulnerability paradoxically intensifies their trust. Chances are they may already know your past, your weakness, your dependence, your cravings, your tendencies, your flaws, your mistakes, your foibles, your regrets. If so, then you have the opportunity to clear up misperceptions and faulty assumptions. You have the opportunity to introduce them to the real you. And importantly teach them the freedom of living authentically.

*Dear Mom and Dad,*

*It was seven o'clock on a Sunday morning when I heard the voice of my mom echo "Time to wake up; we don't want to be late for Sunday mass." You see, this was the day that my loving mother left a big imprint in my heart, an imprint that I will always carry with me for the rest of my life!*

*I was seven years old that Sunday when my mom volunteered me to play in the Sunday church music group. At first I was very nervous and afraid; there was also a part of me that was excited to learn how to play the guitar. As the Sundays passed I became quite the guitar player, some sheet reading but mostly following my instructor's lead and playing the chords by ear. I will never forget the joy and happiness I saw in my mother's eyes every Sunday when she would look over at me from the choir section as if to say, "My Son, I am very proud of you!" As the years passed my mom encouraged me to join a local band performing in small weddings,*

*Church functions and retreats. I loved playing in the band, I loved music; however, it wasn't until my freshmen year in high school that things began to change. It was my Dad; he did not want me to continue down the path of being in a band. There was much angst and resentment bottled up in my father because of my guitar playing. I remember my father would comment about how being a musician would amount to only drinking and drugs, and that school was where I needed to focus. I remember long and late arguments between him and Mom over my music. In fact every time there was a disagreement between him and Mom, I would somehow get brought up and Dad would warn Mom that it will be her fault if I should start drinking and get involved with drugs. I began to feel angry, hurt and most of all I began to feel responsible for the critical, disapproving words my Mom was experiencing, all because of me and my music. I had many watery eyed conversations with my mom as she always encouraged me and asked me not to pay any attention to what was going on.*

*I graduated from high school and on to college I went. I'll never forget the words my mom and father said to me when they said their good-bye's at the airport – "We are so proud of you" meant the world to me. In college I finally understood what my father was really trying to say to me. I was introduced to a young rock band, which I really liked, and wanted to join their group. The band guys were all very nice; however, much to my surprise, not only were they heavy into drugs and drinking, the average age group was about eighteen years old. These were four teens who had dropped out of school and started down the life my dad warned me about. They wanted me to go on the road with them, and although I did not want to admit it, I kept hearing the voice of my father over and over again until I reached a point of peace in my heart – I GOT IT!*

*Music is still a very big part of my life. It became clear to me that both of my parents wanted to give me this gift, just delivered the message differently, as best as they knew how. Thank you, Mom & Dad. Your loving son, Joseph*

When storytelling, don't avoid the tension and the tragedy. Our natural tendency is to pass over the painful disclosure, sugarcoat our aching, cover up the sting, exaggerate the bliss. It's in our vulnerability that grandchildren know more than the name of their grandfather. Without stories we may ignorantly tease his stinginess. But his inescapable story reveals a buried hardship living with seven siblings and a widowed mother; starving and packed in a tiny one-bedroom house with little heat, a shared toothbrush and holed shoes in the dead of Minnesota winters; shooting squirrels for food; pangs of hunger keeping him from concentrating in school; enrolling in the armed forces to break away. Lives that are normal and predictable don't hold our attention. Realness does. Realness reveals the hidden heroic journeys in our family. Realness bares the brokenness and the bravery. It's in our openness that life lessons, not biographies, are passed on. It's in our vulnerability that the mortar is adjoined with family; the stones fuse together and inexorable bonding takes place.

Adversity introduces us to ourselves. When our dignity is assaulted, we are introduced to ourselves. When we are shamed, we are introduced to ourselves. When we are betrayed, we are introduced to ourselves. We grow when the circumstances demand it. Hardship introduces us to inner transformation; it puts us on stage in gripping, heart-pounding, fist-pumping scenes. Good stories tell of the tension between desire (expectations) and tragedy (cruel reality). There is tension and tragedy in your story...in *every* story. It's undeniable. It's inevitable. It's horrific. It's painful and unnerving. But it's also not the ending. Let them see there's a bigger picture. Circumstances don't write our story, especially not the ending. We are responsible for writing our own story. You can't change your tragedy, but you can write a new plot and begin carving story-stones with a purposeful legacy in mind for your family. Let them see your vulnerability turned into victory through your stories.

*Dear Natalie and Ally,*

*This year marks the 20th anniversary of the end of my walk-on football experience at UGA. Though I left Athens somewhat bitter (I guess two ACL surgeries and no playing time will do that to you), I now realize my experience there was more valuable than I ever could have imagined. Who knew that the decision not to quit, after my position coach Dicky Clark shot me straight and said, "You are not going to get playing time but we want you to stick it out. We are going to 'letter' you and 10 years from now, no one will remember or care how much or how little you played, simply being a Bulldog will be enough." I left that meeting, angry to say the least, and called my dad to tell him I was quitting. He listened, didn't really try to talk me out of it, and we hung up. For some reason, I didn't quit. My grades ended up being good enough to make the "Academic all-SEC" team which I thought nothing of; after all, what do grades have to do with football? Fast forward to today, I have a platform to encourage young people to never quit, even if it's not working out the way you planned. I learned something about myself that I would carry to this day – that I will never quit, regardless of how tough it gets. God had bigger plans for my experience than a little playing time! I saw Dicky Clark last year and personally thanked him for telling me the truth, but also providing a glimmer of hope. He was right all along; I just had to be 40, not 20, to understand! Love, Dad*

*But, Then Encouragement.* You don't think anyone wants to hear your story, but they do. You don't think they want to hear the stories of your abandonment, but they need to because they will face betrayal. You don't think they want to know about you bullied, teased to tears, wrongly judged, but they will inevitably feel like an outsider. You don't think they want to hear about your brokenness, but they need to because they will eventually get hurt. The day you got the phone call. The day your distraction caught up with you. The day you felt drained, bare, empty. The day you felt exposed and naked. They need to hear about the day you felt your life was toxic. The day you felt not good enough. The day you reached a dead end. The day you almost quit. The day you almost stopped dreaming. They need to hear about the time in your life when you thought your story was over. Then they need to hear about the hero in you, the transformation, the re-dedication. They need to hear that it gets better. That it feels like you are living for the first time, breathing for the first time, seeing for the first time. Your family needs to be encouraged by your "but, then" life-changes.

> *But, then I decided to . . .*
> *But then I stopped . . .*
> *But, then God . . .*

Tell your family about how you stopped building a wall to protect your broken heart, but then let others inside. Tell your family about how you stopped running away from your life's messiness, but then a miraculous experience drew you to run to your faith. Tell your family about how you stopped achieving your way for others to love you, but then started loving yourself. Tell them about how your life was shattered, broken to pieces, messy without a place to start, but then your sister, your brother, your aunt or uncle pulled you from the wreckage. Tell your family about the imprisonment of living a counterfeit life and pretending on the outside, but then the glorious freedom in being known. Your family needs your stories for guidance, for strength, for validation. Your words can make a difference. So before you begin to write – is your heart in the right place? Is it pure? Is it authentic and vulnerable? Is it focused on your ego or growing others?

*3.4 Quarry Questions*

1. *What do you need to be vulnerable about with your family so an important life lesson is taught?*

2. *We can carry regret around our entire lives and it owns us. What regret owns you? Are you prepared to let it go through storytelling?*

3. *Write down experiences in your Legacy Letter journal when you faced adversity.*

4. *Did you ever bully someone physically or relationally? Did you ever gossip to hurt someone? Were you ever bullied?*

*3.4 Legacy Letters*

1. *Tell a story that makes you feel a little vulnerable. Let someone read it to get comfortable with exposing your vulnerability.*

2. *Write a story about a time when you faced adversity in (3) above. What did you learn about yourself?*

3. *Write a story about a time when your heart was broken.*

4. *Tell a story when you built a wall around yourself for protection. What was the catalyst? What did you learn about yourself?*

### Storytelling with Positivity

When we build our legacy, when we tell our stories, positivity counts. Build your family legacy with joyfulness. Write with a spirit of positivity and gratitude. Promote cheerfulness and contentment. Happiness counts in storytelling.

We have all experienced periods in our lives when we were flourishing – engaged at work, intentional with our families, having a sense of purpose, celebrating what is good, experiencing and giving spontaneous kindness and creativity, bouncing back from setbacks and feeling resilient. We had a certain zest for life. It turns out that researchers are beginning to understand why. Scientists have found that only about 10% of the variance in our individual happiness can be attributed to differences in individuals' life situations like wealth, fame, health, beauty. About half is predetermined genetically, something called a set-point. About 40% is ascribed by our "intentional activities" – how we think, what we do. It turns out that happiness is a choice. Cultural wisdom tells us that if we work hard, we will be more successful and then we will be happy. So we strive to get to that next promotion, win that big deal to get a new car, lose ten pounds before the family reunion, date the beautiful girl in 7A. Scientists have shown that in reality these bring us a little happiness over a short time, but it is not lasting.

---

"For untold generations, we have been led to believe that happiness orbited around success. That if we work hard enough, we will be successful and only if we are successful will we become happy. Now, thanks to breakthroughs in the burgeoning field of positive psychology, we are learning that the opposite is true. Happiness is the center, and success revolves around it."
— Sonya Lyubomirsky, The Happiness Advantage

---

The myth that money brings us a lot of happiness is not entirely true. Large studies have found only a slight increase in happiness levels of executive millionaires compared to their office staff or blue collar workers. "Materialism has been shown to be a strong predictor of unhappiness," says Sonya Lyubomirsky in The Happiness Advantage. In fact, longitudinal studies show that happiness was higher in 1940 with lower quality of life (less education, fewer cars and televisions, and lower salary) than today with all our material advantages. Remember the elation of your new car, the swagger driving to work, proudly parking in your driveway instead of your garage. Co-workers and friends ask you for a ride. Over time the euphoria dissipates. Then someone else gets the newest model and a new swell of covetousness overtakes your now vanquished satisfaction. You have just experienced hedonic adaptation. Creeping normalcy and rising expectations along with social comparison cause us to amass more of what we desire, but overall happiness tends to stay the same. "The bad news about hedonic adaptation is that it ultimately dampens your happiness and satisfaction after any positive event or uplift," says Sonya Lyubomirsky in The Happiness Advantage. So constantly looking outside ourselves to boost our happiness – money, gadgets, beautification, promotion, dating the hunk, gambling wins, video game levels completed – isn't anything more than an immediate jolt without enduring enamor.

---

"Happiness fuels success, not the other way around."
— Sonya Lyubomirsky, The Happiness Advantage

---

Waiting for IF/WHEN events simply lulls us into a false illusion of circumstances regulating our happiness. So we wander around aimlessly, bumbling from purchase to purchase looking for things to boost our happiness. Dr. Barbara Fredrickson, Professor of the Positive Emotions and Psychophysiology Lab at the University of North Carolina, found that people who "flourish" have something in common: they all experience more positivity than negativity in their everyday lives. In 2005 Fredrickson published an article in American Psychologist suggesting that positivity ratios (positive: negative feelings, emotions, comments, perceptions) above about 3-to-1 and below about 11-to-1 are what humans need to flourish. A meta-analysis of happiness research that collated results from over 200 studies involving nearly 275,000 people found that happiness leads to success in nearly every domain of our lives – marriage, health, friendships, careers, community involvement.

Positivity builds inner strengths such as resilience, optimism, acceptance, openness, and purpose.

Happy people live longer – up to ten years longer. Positivity builds physical health. It lowers stress hormones, increases dopamine, and stimulates their immune system.

Positivity builds good mental habits such as perseverance, concentration, mindfulness, problem solving, visual attention, and verbal creativity. Students do better on standardized tests if they feel positive emotions before taking the exams.

Positivity builds social relationships. It strengthens bonds and makes us attractive to others. Positive people experience less loneliness, are more forgiving, and feel less isolated.

We need to increase the quantity of positivity in our life. That's why your storytelling should have the right balance of positivity – it has huge fringe benefits to your family as well as your mind, body, and spirit. Gratitude is a powerful storytelling approach, cultivated with a regular practice of affirming goodness and then sharing our appreciation with others. Studies show that just writing down five things you are grateful for once a week increases happiness by 25 percent. Gratitude can be a booster shot for relationships. One study found that couples expressing gratitude to each other resulted in increased connectedness and satisfaction in their relationship the next day. Studies are finding that gratitude matters to kids too. A University of California-Berkeley study found that teens who had high levels of gratitude entering high school had less negative emotions and episodes of depression; those with more positive emotions had greater life satisfaction and happiness four years later when they were finishing school. We need to be more explicit with our gratitude. How many family members, co-workers, friends know you are grateful for them?

*Dear Jonathan, Nicholas, and Rachel,*

*Never forget to say "thank you." I don't just mean politely. I mean unsolicited with immense gratitude for those who gave you so much. One of my favorite stories in the Bible was when Jesus healed the ten lepers. Lepers were required to live outside the community because of the contagiousness of the disease. Leprosy left people disfigured. Brothers and sisters, sons and daughters, moms and dads were outcast from their community and pariahs to their family. Imagine people running away from you fearful of getting too close. Ten lepers begged Jesus to heal them; they called to Him from a distance. He instructed them to show themselves to the priests. As they walked toward the Temple, they were healed. Only one returned to Jesus – a Samaritan! Don't you think the other nine were thankful too? After years of being outsiders because of massive skin lesions that made them look like "monsters," don't you think they were thrilled, elated, exuberant, ecstatic? They were made new, a life do-over. But they never went back to say thanks. They were thankful alright, but it went unexpressed. I'm just as culpable; I think we all are . . . to bosses and co-workers, to moms and dads, to brothers and sisters, to friends and neighbors. Every year at Thanksgiving I send three notes out to people for which I haven't wholly expressed my gratitude. One year I sent it to a boss who took a chance on me with an undeserved, early promotion. One year I sent it to a co-worker who put a mirror to my face on a leadership blind spot. One year I sent it to my brother who encouraged me to start-up my nutrition business when I was chicken. Every year I send one to your mom because she is wonderful in so many ways that go unnoticed. Don't let unexpressed gratitude rob someone of the joy of knowing they were appreciated; give a "thank you" to those who gave to you. Love, Dad.*

*Find positive meaning in your experiences.* Positivity doesn't need to be at odds with a pure heart. Being authentic and real is paramount. Writing with positivity doesn't mean we have a gullible approach to our real tragedies or sugarcoat the hurt in our lives. But we should be mindful in the aggregate of the positive-to-negative ratio of our stories.

We can lean toward having our stories even the score, underscore others' bad behavior, sling mud, but such self-serving stories don't provide useful stones for legacy building. Our stories shouldn't be about judging or criticizing others – *our stories are not for helping you address relationship tensions.* Does it enrich future generations in your family to know what a dirty liar your uncle was? Probably not. Does it enrich future generations in your family to know how your grandmother's bias toward her grandchildren hurt you? Unlikely. Better stories recount the grace of forgiving hurtful relationships that caused you to cry yourself to sleep. Better stories overcome those dark corners in your life where you are harboring resentment, where the light of forgiveness exposed something beautifully unexpected in you and undeserved for someone else. Better stories tell about the transformation, the restoration, the upheaval, the choice "that it ends here."

## 3.5 Quarry Questions

1. *Look over the Ten Forms of Positivity – Joy, Gratitude, Serenity, Interest, Hope, Pride, Fun, Inspiration, Awe, Love. Which do you experience most/least often? Review the list and think about a time when you experienced this form of positivity. Write stories about how you see these forms of positivity in your children.*

2. *Practice gratitude by keeping a gratitude journal. Every day jot down at least three things you are grateful for and why. Use these as story starters.*

3. *What are times when someone noticed something you needed and then provided you with it? What are some things someone gave up for you?*

*3.5 Legacy Letters*

1. *Write unexpressed gratitude letters to family, friends, co-workers who had helped you but whom you never properly thanked.*

2. *What careless words did you tell someone and deeply regret it? What unspoken words of affirmation need to be told to your family in a story?*

### Storytelling that Prompts

Throughout our lives we 'try on' different narratives prompted by culture, friends, or family. We see what "fits" – does it feel natural, do I attain any social benefit, does it feel consistent with my self-image? If you like how it fits, then you'll decide to wear that "persona outfit" again, sometimes over an entire lifetime. These narratives help us make sense of ourselves, establish a pattern of behaviors and attitudes, and eventually form a self-identity.

Positive self-perceptions propel a self-enhancing cycle. The more you see yourself as kind, the more you will act to be helpful. The more you see yourself as a developer of people, the more available you are to mentor. The more your children see themselves as mutual guardians responsible for each other, the more they will protect each other's hearts. Imagine the incredible potential energy formed in our kids and grandkids with instilled positive self-perceptions. But the same is true with negative perceptions. The more you see yourself as unlovable, the more you withdraw from relationships. The more you see yourself as "not smart," the more you give up academically or artificially set a lid on your potential. Imagine how self-narratives – what they say, do, believe about themselves – shape and mold their character and self-image.

Our stories prompt self-perceptions; it's not just *what* we write about but *how* we write that has consequences for their self-perception. Think about how over-generalizations and narrow self-perceptions about a person can influence their life. You can almost anticipate the

wrong-turns, the self-talks in the mirror, the diary letters, the calcified relationships, the withdraw from life.

> *"She is a loner and isn't fun."*
> *"She's smart, but not pretty."*
> *"She's pretty, but not smart."*
> *"He's just not the marrying type."*
> *"She's never going to find someone."*
> *"He's always had problems with commitment."*
> *"He's always had a difficult time completing things."*
> *"She's always been trouble."*
> *"He's always had trouble with anger and rage."*

We all have had such over-generalizations fastened to us and we all
have believed them. Maybe not wholly, maybe not completely, but even
fractionally the scars are noticeable. We have felt the gravitational pull
of them elusively having sway in our lives. We can see in retrospect that
we filter life experiences according to them. The twisted beliefs set into
erroneous, durable vows. *I'll never . . . I'll always . . .* We reach conclusions
about ourselves that are self-deprecating lies, over-generalizations that
are just too narrow and don't include enough nuances, angles, lenses,
reinterpretations. Such perceptions create a definition for ourselves and
this can influence the paths we choose. Often there is little evidence for
our over-generalizations, but they affect us deeply and the stinging hurt
can be difficult to shake. And it affects how we build a legacy for our
family. When I was a kid I believed over-generalizations that triggered
skewed self-characterizations and self-told lies.

*You have no common sense.* I avoided circumstances that didn't require deep analytical thinking. I worried in social situations that I'd
say something foolish.

*You have to fix your acne or you'll never get a girlfriend.* As a teen,
young single adult, and eventually newlywed, I saw ugliness in the
mirror that precipitated fear of abandonment.

*There's a black cloud hanging over me.* I'd over-dramatize the negative events in my life and pessimistically see life as a half-empty glass. At first, people would find my joking entertaining, but eventually the sullenness frayed my working, social, and family relationships.

Language is not innocent. The labels we carry with us define our identity. We take these labels into our work lives, into our family relationships, and into our spirituality. We are all wearing self-fulfilling labels that say, "Hello, My Name is _____ and I'm _____." Kids live up or live down to their labels. If you look close enough, you can see the labels affixed to people, you can see the badges your family wears – "ugly," "geek," "sucks at sports," "stupid," "lazy," "chicken," "selfish," "angry," "courageous," "thoughtful," "considerate," "kind," "generous," "clever," "honest," "cheerful," "mentor," "helpful," "gentle," "sweet," "giver," "loyal," "trustworthy." If we don't think twisted, harmful labels matter, consider the dramatic scores of young girls who cut themselves. A 2008 longitudinal study at Yale University found that 36% of girls engaged in non-suicidal self-injury within the past year, as much as 56% during their lifetime. The single best antidote for the poison of negative labels is ensuring children develop a strong sense of self. Our storytelling can put labels on them before others do.

We are in a race to develop the core narratives in our family before culture distorts their self-image. We are in a contest to shape the core narratives of our family before social media creates self-made stigmas. We are in rivalry to affix true labels on their image and their heart. So without positive prompting from parents, our kids see themselves as fat, stupid, ugly, gross, unworthy of friends, and a litany of other insults that infect and disease their self-image. If we don't prompt, then someone else will. They are wearing labels right now – at school, on the field, at their work, at their home, on a date. Whose voice are they listening to and believing? Self-enhancing labels aligned with your family's core values can shield them from peer labels that see bullying as cool, or being sexually alluring as popular, or sucker-punching others as funny, or ostracizing others as entertaining. A close, trusting relationship with you can immunize them from self-deprecating whispers.

We have the ability to prompt the core narratives of our children – directing new ways of explaining and understanding themselves. The implicit beliefs and regard our family has for each other directs their self-narrative. We can reinforce a positive, self-enhancing narrative. Overtly noticing your daughter being particularly generous and responding with, "Look at you being so unbelievably generous," tells her that this behavior *fits* her . . . Maybe she should try it on again. And after a while, it may become a facet of her core narrative. She may start identifying herself as "a generous person." And her behaviors will follow – in her family, in her work, in her community.

*Dear Rachel,*

*As early as 18 months, Mom and I saw something inside you. Before you were able to put words and sentences together, we saw a deep spirit of kindness, a heart of gold. Sometimes it just takes my breath away – when you generously share your two cookies with your brothers, when you generously give sandbox toys to hoarding peers, when you spontaneously give hugs when someone needs it the most. In first grade, you boldly raised your hand on the first day of school to help a little girl who didn't know English. In third grade, you raced dead last with a student who struggled to finish, and your vigor and kindheartedness encouraged her when she felt defeated. I marvel at how selfless you are.*

*In a world that seems so focused on getting, I'm so proud of how giving you are. Embrace it. Protect it. Pursue it. Nurture it. Don't ever let it go. It's what makes you so special. Sometimes it will feel like your heart will break, but He made it so it won't. Countless lives will be grateful, many without ever saying "thank you." Don't let that discourage you. Besides, you don't help because you want the recognition, you do it because you care and love. Know that every act of kindness is a drop that fills someone's vessel. I know because you place drops in my vessel every day until it overflows. Love, Dad*

Encourage family by noticing their positive attitudes and behaviors. Let them know that you see it fitting nicely on them like a beautiful dress or a clean, crisp shirt. Let them know that they look stunning in it. *When you did that, I was speechless . . . couldn't stop telling your mom . . . was so proud of you . . . made my week . . .* With loving approval, prompt them to see the events in their lives not just as random circumstances, but extraordinary opportunities to place their fingerprints, to touch with a silver lining, to grow into the kind of men or women they aspire to be. Prompt them make a difference over being different, strive for significance over social success.

---

"Children are like wet cement. Whatever falls on them makes an impression." — Dr. Haim Ginott

---

Sometimes events need re-interpreting, perceptions need to be changed, and frames of reference need to be broken. This is particularly true of negativity that creates a self-defeating cycle of skewed perceptions and behaviors. Story prompting can redirect the disoriented. What passing comments have stuck with you to this day? Insecurity is a poison. It can paralyze us. The antidote for insecurity is acceptance. The trajectory of our kids' relationships is highly determined by their acceptance or rejection in our home. This shapes their hearts and it ripples across family generations. Let your kids know that you rely on them. Let them see you cheering them on in life. Let them know that you believe in them. Let them know that you wholly accept their physical, mental, and personality makeup. Let your kids know unequivocally that you love them – all of them including the idiosyncrasies. Don't let them infer it; tell them. Carve some stones for them to see.

We are wired to seek acceptance. We don't find friends; we are attracted to those that accept us. We naturally gravitate to people who accept us – boyfriends and girlfriends, high school circles and college hang-outs. Our kids will try to fill the acceptance void by wandering to and fro among groups and self-characterizations until they find it. Isn't it true that the head shaking circle of friends in high school accepted you when others didn't? Isn't it true that the circle of now lifelong friends in college accepted you first? Isn't it true that your head-in-hands old boyfriend really wasn't a great choice to complete you? He certainly didn't adore you, but he accepted you when others didn't. Your family is wired for acceptance; at any age we are parental acceptance magnets. Dr. Jean Twenge, professor of psychology at San Diego State University, has been studying the growing prevalence of anxiety in the US. Dr. Twenge in "The Age of Anxiety" examined sixteen different factors that drive anxiety in women. Social trust is the highest predicator of anxiety – more than unemployment or economic conditions or marital strife. Your family needs to have a profound trust in you – that you have their back; that they can lean on you when they are weak; that you will stand with them battling through life; that you will hold their hand when they need tender love.

As master builders we are called to breathe affirmation into our children. Our kids never outgrow this. Let your kids know that you need them too. When my daughter was about three, I started a cute little routine. I'd walk around the house a little downcast, despondent, unhappy – a different persona from my usual positive perkiness. "What's wrong, Daddy?" "I could really use a hug from my Rachel." She would burst on the scene and proudly give me a warm embrace. Then I'd *show her* with exaggerated facial expressions. "This is what I was like before you gave me a hug" . . . lifeless, stoic, demure face. "This is what I feel like now" . . . beaming bright smile. She was so pleased with herself. She knew that I need her too – her protector, her provider, her dad relies on her too. During an event at her school, each child needed to answer questions about their dad and themselves –one of the questions was, "What superpowers do you have?' Rachel wrote, "My hugs make my dad feel good inside smile no matter what." Over the years, the routine lost some of its flare, causing her to roll her eyes and blurt, "Oh really, Dad." But I still do it as a reminder that her special embrace is always meaningful to me no matter her age.

---

"There is a misperception that people need fixing and modern psychology has promoted this. The problem with psychology in the twentieth century was to think that people are pushed by the past, instead of thinking that they are pulled by the future."
— Dr. Seligman, author of Learned Optimism and expert of positive psychology

---

What if how you introduced your son or daughter or grandson or granddaughter actually became what they strived for; what if they lived up to it? What if how you believed in them became self-fulfilling? What if you revealed what longings you had for them, what you hoped for in them, what qualities you admired in them? We live up to the honor of our introductions.

*Dear Jonathan,*

*When you were in fourth grade, you did something extraordinary, something that as an adult, I struggle with – standing up and standing alone for what you believe in, even when it comes at a personal cost. A developmentally challenged boy in your class befriended you. You were kind and considerate to him – often staying behind during recess in the classroom waiting for him to finish his work. He shadowed you like a big brother. On the playground some boys were mean to him – making fun of his mannerisms and awkward phrases. You defended him and then you were targeted, bullied, and ostracized. You hated going to school. You couldn't understand how kids could be so malicious and turn from friends to haters. When the intimidation escalated, we talked to you about switching classrooms or schools. You astonished us – "How could I ever leave Stephen?" You were so brave; you were a hero to your friend. I hope you always see yourself as a selfless, just man who defends the needs of others regardless of the personal cost. Love, Dad*

Prompt them to live lives worthy of stories that want to be repeated over and over again in your family.

### 3.6 Quarry Questions

1. *What labels are you wearing (both positive and negative)? Where did they come from?*

2. *What careless words calcified unfair insecurities in you?*

3. *What labels are your children wearing? What false narratives are your children vulnerable to believing from culture and society?*

4. *Collect stories from people in all contexts and circumstances in your life by asking them to describe your best labels. Do the same for your family members. Create positive self-portraits and use it to remove negative self-perceptions.*

### 3.6 Legacy Letters

1. *What positive prompts do your children need to hear from you? Tell them in a story.*

2. *Tell your family a story about a label you had worn for a long time (or still are wearing).*

3. *What labels do you want your children to wear? What positive narratives need to be protected? Write stories reflecting how you see these qualities in your children and grandchildren.*

4. *Tell your family the story behind their pet names.*

## Storytelling with Perspective

Your stories were meant to be told and your legacy is meant to be built with your stories. Listen to your own story. Connect the dots. See the patterns and the breath-taking scenes. Your story has unique characters, surprising plot twists, themes, tension and suspense, tragedy and redemption, surpassing joy and deep embraces, tearful goodbyes and heart-pounding starts, awe-stricken spiritual moments, and wide-eyed beginnings. In the moment we can't see the sweeping drama unfold in your life, over generations. We need to see with a wider horizon and a different vantage point.

---

"Our story begins with the characters who gave us birth, including past relationships with their parents and issues such as success and shame; power and abuse; love, loss and addiction; heartache and secrets; and family myths. Our birth is a beginning, but we owe our existence to the generations that came before us. Our beginning, which took place before we were born, signals some of the themes that will play out in our life." — Dr. David Allender, To Be Told

---

*Different versions of the same story.* There are different versions to our stories seen through contrasting angles and perspectives. When we write stories, we need to understand that we often write from a singular perspective that has hidden biases, assumptions and "baggage" from the past. It's not wrong, but often it's a narrow view that requires us to look in the mirror and see circumstances from other angles. Every story has a vantage that defines the perspective, and your perspective creates a specific version to the story.

The same events can be storytold in different ways. One college summer I spent surveying a northern Wisconsin lake to create a topographic map of the lake and the surrounding area. A boat would traverse the lake with a depth finder at a constant speed then raise a flag every 60–90 seconds. Students manning transits on the shoreline would at that flag-raising moment record a bearing. When we collected all of the data, we always needed at least three intersecting lines to pinpoint an accurate location. When we storytell we often have a single vantage and it's highly influenced by our schemas. Consider writing a version of your story by triangulating multiple vantages. We can broaden what we choose to look for and listen to in our lives, to see alternative versions so we have a richer depiction of ourselves and our experiences. Take an event in your life . . . How would three people who may be part of the story see it differently? All three are true stories to each person. Which one is truer? It's important to reinterpret episodes in life, to step back, examine them, reframe them. Take another event in your life . . . How would you write about the event at the moment, a week later, several years or even decades later? All are true stories. Which one is truer? Alternative versions of the same event change the story and the message. Which one of these stories is truer?

- Someone sees: Alarm clock buzzing for an eternity. A mom rolls out of bed disheveled. Late night. The house is disorganized. Breakfast is on-the-go after too much time bathing her daughter because she didn't bathe before bed. Everyone leaves hurried with a brown bag lunch.

- Someone else sees: My mom stayed up late packing a homemade lunch for me after she finished helping my brother with his math homework. I peeked inside to see if I could find the note from Mom "hidden" somewhere. I rushed to the school bus because Mom was helping me pick out something to wear today.

- Someone else sees: My mom helped me figure out my Algebra homework when I was just so frustrated and down on myself. I thought that I was stupid with math, but it turns out to be tricky even for my mom . . . We figured it out together late last night with a cup of hot cocoa. She's awesome with that. I left for school this morning confident for the first time in weeks.

Curing time matters in writing your stories. Some writing may not have bow-tied endings or tight conclusions. In fact many stories unfold over years and sometimes over generations. Learn to watch your story unfold beautifully over time. Look for patterns and connections not just in your life, but in others' lives – mom and dad, siblings, grandparents, great-grandparents.

Getting the perspective right in our storytelling isn't just about accuracy. The perspective on how we narrate about ourselves has a big impact not just on how others see us and the wisdom we leave them, but also how *we* think, how *we* feel, how *we* see ourselves. How we narrate about ourselves creates expectations, and our interpretation of episodes in our life can determine how we think, act, and believe. Writing from multiple vantages doesn't suggest choosing the best one to storytell. But it is important to understand that the story version matters not only in transferring the lesson (your purpose), but also in establishing the narrative (your positivity and pure heart).

---

"The stories we tell about our lives are not simply accounts of experiences, they also generate experiences: how we feel, what we think, what possibilities and obstacles we see for ourselves."
— Positive Identities

---

*Get in the habit of touchstoning your stories.* In ancient Greece touchstones – a black siliceous stone – were used to assay precious metals. Drawing a line with metals on a touchstone leaves a visible trace. Different alloys of gold and other precious metals have different colors, so unknown samples can be compared to samples of known purity. Check the genuineness of your stories by using a trusted friend, contemplation and prayer as a touchstone. We should elicit the help of others in writing our story. Who are our co-authors? Have these people co-write or at least have them in mind as your write (figuratively sitting beside you), otherwise we can be writing with a distorted lens of ourselves and our circumstances. When story writing, look *around* the event – circumstances leading to it and the aftermath in hindsight. Don't rush to conclusions without surveying the story from multiple angles and perhaps from the vantage of other people. How did your brother see the same circumstances? How did your cousin perceive that summer? Consider a few vantages across time and personas to triangulate your story; then write with a simple, singular message.

*Dear Jonathan, Nicholas, and Rachel,*

*We spent many summers camping in Maine as kids. One year we hiked throughout most of Acadia National Park. I'll never forget one trail in particular – The Precipice. It wasn't the distance or the steep inclines, but the drop-offs that made my knees weak. It was the first time I'd seen my dad afraid for his three young teens and the first time I remember being afraid for my less-than-agile dad. We cautiously ascended narrow trails and steep drops holding tightly to iron hand rails and parallel iron foot rails. We often considered giving up as the summit was hidden from our view and the dangers ahead were unforeseen. I can still remember the exhilaration of safely reaching the top with a stunning vista of the rugged seacoast. I've carried a few lessons from The Precipice with me on journeys – professional and recreational – throughout my life. Take along companions that have your back and encourage you when you feel weak. Our youngest brother Mark was the can-do voice that propelled us up the mountain. Be careful of the descent from the top; it can often be more dangerous because you are complacent and inattentive. Love, Dad*

*Stories have a time and place.* Some stories can be read and repeated often. Many other stories have a timetable for telling. Explaining the first time you felt awkward, different, or like an outsider is glaringly relevant to a middle schooler. Telling of your butterflies several days before your first date can be comforting to your awkward high schooler. Unfolding the painful eroding of relationship and closeness with your parents from chronic lying – invaluable to youngsters. Explaining to your sluggish son the exhilaration of your first paycheck and the freedom in having money to buy your own things (including that one thing you always wanted) – poignantly pertinent. Telling your daughter, now an impetuous, rookie manager, the joy of developing an employee into a top-performer – foundational for finding satisfaction in her career. Recounting the emotional heartache and jealousy scars of premarital sex – highly relevant for your teen son or daughter. Witnessing your sister crumble under the devastation of marriage infidelity – relevant for your thirty-something kids. Write your stories with a timetable perspective for telling.

*Dear Ashley, Nicholas, and Natalie:*

*From my discussions with each of you I know that you want to make good decisions about how to best use the financial resources that are being entrusted to you through your careers and ventures. These decisions – those that involve the money we make – can be some of the hardest and most emotional decisions we have to make for our families. And, regardless of whether those financial choices are good or bad, what's certain is they will leave a lasting impact on your family. You see, the financial decisions we make are truly like foot prints we leave behind, foot prints that most likely will be followed by our children. Footprints that if we choose wisely can help guide our children toward a path to a healthy financial lifestyle that will support a strong family.*

*I hope that each of you recognizes that as you were growing up your mother and I made a purposeful decision to stick by a few key financial core values . . . "We will always spend less than we make"; "We will give to our church"; "We will make sure our* kids receive a high quality education without incurring debt"; and "Our home mortgage will be our only debt." Sometimes we did make financial mistakes and your mother and I did have disagreements about what was or was not in keeping with those values. But, ultimately, we found our way back to the path and reaffirmed these four values that have largely guided the financial decisions we have made.

Your mom and I were fortunate that we didn't have to figure out these principles all on our own. We had some great teachers and mentors along the way that helped shape our financial views. One of the most impactful of these has been your Grandma Betty and Grandpa Bob. I remember being blown away when I first learned from your mother how generous Grandma and Grandpa were with their local church and a vast host of missionaries serving all over the world that they sponsored. Your Grandma and Grandpa cheerfully lived well below their means driving older cars, ensuring they had no debt but a small mortgage, and being sure to share their blessings with others all along the way. We learned they had great role models in their parents who also were generous and lived financially conservative lives.

Seeing your Grandma and Grandpa live a life of Godly financial stewardship gave your mom and me the courage to try to follow from the start of our marriage. I know you kids sometimes wished we could have had a newer car, that you had more trendy clothes, a cell phone earlier, or could have gone on nicer vacations or that you received a bigger allowance. All of these things probably would have been nice, but I hope you agree that they really were not all that important to our family's happiness and well-being in the long term.

Each of you may make different choices than we have made. But, I hope that whatever choices you make about yours and your *family's finances that they will be well thought out and supported by much discussion and prayer, and; that you will stick to those decisions that are working even when life and circumstances tempt you to deviate from the path of Godly financial steward-ship. I love you very much! Dad*

## 3.7 Quarry Questions

1. *Choose a tenuous event in your life and see it from different van-tages. Write down how you perceived the event during, one week later, one month later, one year later. Write down the perspective of others who were part of the experience.*

2. *What are the little moments, the lasting impressions just between you and your dad, between you and your mom, between you and your grandparents? A furtive look from dad when you were trying to get away with something; a deep embrace from mom when you least expected it, but needed it the most; Dad's arm around your shoulder; a calm, assured tone from Mom; the smell of grandpa's aftershave when he would lift you up off the ground; the calls and care packages in college.*

## 3.7 Legacy Letters

1. *Write about a time when your perspective changed with the passage of time or listening to (not judging) the perception of others. What did you learn about patiently waiting for your perspective to come into focus?*

2. *Write a story about being just in the right place at the right time.*

3. *Write a story about a time when you enthusiastically said "yes" to something that you later wished you had said "no."*

### *Storytelling with Pulse and Presence*

Your storytelling needs your presence. Write as if you are telling the story right there – with a chair pulled up to your daughter's bed, with your arm wrapped around your son's shoulders, with your hands clasped in your mom's hands, with your head in your hands, fallen on your knees, jumping up and down. Imagine sitting down eye to eye with your great-grandson. Cuddled underneath a blanket with your granddaughter. Hiking along a trail with your son and stopping at the stream to throw stones. Write as if you are staring into your daughter's big brown eyes. Write with long pauses. Enunciate. Repeat phrases. Write with a crackled voice and blurred vision, tears on the paper, sweaty palms, deafening silence, clenched jaw, bitten nails. Write with breathless desperation. Write with shouted joy. Write with a whisper. Write with passion. Write with pulse.

*Not Just Telling, But Feeling Your Story. How* do you tell your story? Your narrative writing should not just tell wisdom, but express it. How do you write about your infidelity, your workaholism, your prodigal years, your co-dependency, your bottom, your yearning as a son/daughter, your turning point as a father, your fear of dependence, your devotion to your spouse, your financial recklessness, your faith journey? Your family doesn't just want you to tell them a story; they want to feel your story. When we *feel* history over telling it, we inseparably connect the storyteller with the listener. When we *feel* history over telling it, it's unmistakably yours.

*Dear Caleb,*

*My heart was broken the day you cried because our family doesn't look like other families. From birth you've always lived with me and visited your dad. Even still, I knew one day you would wonder why this was our reality. From the time you were in the womb, I mourned the day you might feel as though you lacked something by not having your dad live with you. I always wanted you to feel confident, firm in your identity. My biggest fear was that you would feel shaken or broken with the realization that our family was different. Like you, I was disappointed that I couldn't give you the kind of upbringing that mirrored my own. I was sad and ashamed of my decision to engage in a relationship with your father before I knew him well enough to marry. Which is why we never did. Raising you in a single-parent home is not at all what I imagined or wanted for you. It took me some time to come to terms with it myself.*

*There are so many lessons in my story, in our story. Lessons I intend to share with you over time and ones that I hope you will carry with you throughout your life. For now, though, I want you to know that you and we are evidence that God is loving and merciful and gracious. Our life has been full of miracles and blessings. As a single parent, I have been able to stay home with you for your first five years. I've been able to really enjoy each stage of your development without distraction. We have traveled domestically and abroad. I've watched the books we've read come to life for you on many old-fashioned road trips. I have enjoyed motherhood in a way that I never imagined I could as a single parent. Only God could make that possible. In the Bible, God says He can do exceedingly abundantly above all that we could ask or think. He has certainly done that for us. While I never imagined having a family like ours, I couldn't have imagined the outpouring of God's love and abundance upon us. In the beginning I thought I would never be able to give you what I had growing up in a two-parent home. What I know now is the life we have is beyond what I'd hoped for. Love, Mommy*

*Mark every stone with your distinctiveness.* Stories say something about us. It has been said that a storyteller does not choose the stories, but the stories choose the teller. The stories you tell and how you tell a story – what you emphasize or dismiss – speak volumes to your audience. Storytellers rely solely on their words to spark visualization.

Stories are uniquely your own; your fingerprints on the world; your marks in the stones of your family's cathedral. Storytelling with presence means being fully known. Not dark secrets, but what flows from your heart.

I can tell about playing high school football – my position, my record, my accolades. Or I can storytell about how it blossomed something dormant inside me; how I found my voice as a leader to motivate and inspire others which I later carried into my career and community; how I thrived being on an underdog team as an underdog player and carried this fierce tenacity throughout my life; how I developed mental and physical toughness playing through the pain of fractured wrists and a separated shoulder; how Coach Colistra, Radvanski and Hyman instilled a gritty can-do attitude in an impressionable teen that I have carried with me beyond the field.

I can list my favorite music and movies or I can storytell about how I'm a big baby. Cry at moving movies – *Gladiator, Braveheart, Remember the Titans, Shawshank Redemption, Chronicles of Narnia, Schindler's List, Brother Bear, Beauty and the Beast, Rocky*; how I cry every Sunday singing worship songs; how I used to hold my emotions in because culture told me it wasn't manly . . . until I was man enough to let it out.

I can tell about saving money or I can storytell about when I was fifteen and inadvertently answered a call for my dad (also named Bruce); how the angry man demanded payment for a credit card bill; how his threats scared me; how frugality permanently permeated my life.

I can tell about my fears – roller-coasters, heights – or I can storytell about when I dreadfully stood on stage with trembling knees in a crowd of hundreds of middle schoolers, and recounted my life as a pretender – wasting my youth pretending to be someone I wasn't because I didn't like who I was; how I kept building lies to make up for what I lacked; how my silent revelry robbed me of joy; how I'd look in the mirror and the man didn't resemble who I wanted to be; how consistent morning devotion pulled me from the rubble of a masquerade life and changed me from the inside out.

I can tell about my global work assignments – traveling to places like Argentina, Vietnam, Australia, Israel, Korea, Thailand, Chile, Colombia, Singapore – or I can storytell about how a trip to India transformed me from a "taker" in my isolated world to a "giver" in this immense world; how I couldn't eat for days seeing the poverty; how I'd give away my meals to the starving street beggars; how dozens of maimed women and children would bang on the window of my taxi; how I fell to my knees in a pool of emotions every night – despair, gratitude, embarrassment, humility.

*Narrate as only you can.* In your voice – not produced, but raw. Not safe or nice, but real, candid, honest. You want your stories to be picked up not just once a lifetime, but throughout a lifetime. Retribution stories won't get recited again. Grandstanding won't get a second read. Stirring their heart will. Authenticity will. Vulnerability will. A pure heart will. Your story should rouse him, bring her to tears of joy, compel him to ask hard questions and examine himself. Your stories should compel them to pick up a hammer and chisel and continue cutting story stones for our family cathedral, for their children and their grandchildren.

*Dear Jonathan, Nicholas, and Rachel,*

*Sometimes life's hardships and pain can seem so meaningless and senseless. The plan for growth after a devastating forest fire is built into every forest. Seeds of the Jack Pine are only opened with the intense heat of the forest fire. I was a workaholic coming fresh off my MBA wanting to prove myself to my co-workers, boss, and myself. I was working from 5 a.m. to 6 p.m. every day, having a quick dinner, and getting back to work. I was insecure in my abilities and lacked self-confidence in my work, so I overcompensated. The downward spiral of exhaustion caused cloudy thinking which required me to work more which fed my tiredness. It wasn't months of discouragement from my boss, or the pleading of Mom that got my attention, but a fender-bender – nearly asleep at the wheel at 5:30 p.m. – just outside my office building that lit a fire for me. Fortunately no one was hurt, but embarrassment smoldered in me for several days. I "re-started" my work-family balance one Monday morning with adequate sleep and clear boundaries – a commitment to leave work at 5 p.m. for dinner with my family every night and never open my briefcase at home. I've been following that resolution with very few exceptions for 15 years. I still accomplished and completed my accountabilities with less hours a week – more spent with you and Mom. No one missed those hours at work, but you would have missed out if I wasn't at home. Sure, there were times when I needed to put in extra time to complete deadlines. But I would go to bed early and get to work early to squeeze in my assignments to be assured that I would have dinner with you. Learn from your forest fires. Let them get your attention, then start anew. Love, Dad*

How we communicate – not the grammar or the punctuation, but the pulse matters immensely. Forget sentence structure – get your presence across to the listener. More than details, pulse transfers the truth of your story. Scientists have proven that emotions can have a powerful impact on memory; emotional stories are likely to be re-called more often and with more clarity than neutral events. Stories that evoke emotions are recalled at the right moment; they are easily repeated and move with our family across the years. "That's what dad meant when he said . . ." Success. "Remember that story mom told us about the time when . . ." Victory. "My grandpa seemed to know this would happen. He told me this story once . . ." Triumph. Family will ultimately make their own decisions. But your story stowed in their mind can be recalled like whispered wisdom at the intersection of hard choices.

*Write your hero's journey.* We all dream of being a legend. There is a false notion that heroism is a scarce commodity – reserved for a predestined few who ride on white horses, wear polished infallible armor, put their lives in danger for beautiful princesses. Generosity is heroic. Serving others is heroic. Kindness is heroic, but it can often be portrayed in culture as wimpy. Heroes in movies are fiercely resolute, powerful, invulnerable, witty, steadfast . . . this is our cultural imprinting. As Sharon Salzberg says in <u>The Force of Kindness</u>, kindness is "always less . . . less smart, less bold, less imposing, less striking, less beautiful. But kindness always uplifts us and others. Kindness always makes a difference. Receiving kindness from others supports our sense of being someone deserving of love, someone who can accomplish things and vanquish difficulties, who can make it through the travails of life . . ." Our life stories aren't isolated events, but connected, yoked, united by an inner transformation; your story is a hero's journey. You don't need to be aristocrasy to be a cherished princess. You don't need to slay dragons to be a hero.

A brother rescuing his sister from cruelty and abuse – a hero's journey.

A daughter caring for her father with Alzheimer's – a hero's journey.

Overcoming alcohol's craving – a hero's journey.

Rescuing your daughter from giving herself to men for acceptance – a hero's journey.

Disabling your controlling tendencies and honoring your spouse – a hero's journey.

Debt-owned to debt-free – a hero's journey.

Adopting a child – a hero's journey.

Beating cancer – a hero's journey.

Losing 30 pounds – a hero's journey.

Spending Thanksgiving preparing food for the less fortunate – a hero's journey.

Reconfirming your wedding vows after being inattentive and distant for years – a hero's journey.

Running to God after years of running away from Him – a hero's journey.

Forgiving your dad for betraying your family – a hero's journey

Never missing your kids' home games – a hero's journey.

A single mom holding two jobs yet always home to help with homework – a hero's journey.

A teen who stands alone against the grain of her friends because their poor decisions are at odds with her beliefs – a hero's journey.

Fostering a child – a hero's journey.

*Dear Mi amor,*

*Since you came into my life I have always been committed and clear to make sure you have a beautiful life filled with health, joy, happiness, companionship and love. Because of this several times in my life I decided not accept or proceed with opportunities that could have been good for me but not the best for both of us. Sometimes this meant not taking a higher role to develop my career path forward, because this would have meant that I would have spent less time with you, when you would have needed me to laugh with you, support you and be there with you when you felt you had a big challenge or perhaps just when you needed to chat about anything with your mom. This has been much more important and meaningful than adding any material assets to our lives. As you advance in life be very clear on what your core values are, be clear on those things that are not negotiable and always stay true to them because they will make your beloved ones happier as well as yourself. Te Amo, Ma*

Look for patterns in your story. Identify your inner transformation in FROM/TO sequences. Poisons to antidotes, wounded to healed, lost to found. It's in these transformations that we can find the hidden hero emblazoned in each of us. It's in these stories that we can inspire our family to see that their moribund circumstances don't determine an ending. Your stories entice your family to persist, to overcome, to conquer, to hope.

From BETRAYAL to LOVE
From CONTROL to TENDERNESS
From ENVY to CONTENTMENT
From ANGER to GRACE
From HEARTBREAK to HEALING
From NEEDY to WORTHY
From WORRY to PEACE
From TORMENTED to CONQUEROR
From EMPTINESS to FULLNESS
From BEATEN to TRIUMPHANT
From ARROGANT to VULNERABLE
From FOLLOWING OTHERS to LEADING YOUR LIFE
From RESENTMENT to FORGIVENESS
From LOST to RETURNED
From CONTROLLED to FREE
From to IRRESPONSIBLE to DEPENDABLE
From PRODIGAL to OBEDIENT

From DESPAIR to HOPE
From THIRSTY to SATISFIED
From TRUSTLESS to TRUSTWORTHY
From IMPOSTER to AUTHENTIC
From HATRED to LOVE

## 3.8 Quarry Questions

1.  *Choose some of your complex story stones and practice using imagery and metaphors for deeper descriptions of your feelings.*

2.  *What events or circumstances beautifully release your emotions? Cause your heart to swell? Cause your stomach to knot? Still a scar? Always make you smile?*

3.  *What are your hero stories as a child, a teen, a young adult, a husband/wife, a mom/dad, a grandfather/grandmother? We journey through life with companions. Who accompanied you along your heroic journeys?*

4.  *Find what's epic in your life – love, danger, unlikely heroic events, romance, sacrifice, insurmountable odds, lifelong friendship. Look for them and ask others to look for them with you – brothers and sisters, aunts and uncles, moms and dads.*

5.  *Make a list of FROM/TO transformations in your life.*

## 3.8 Legacy Lessons

1.  *Encourage kindness by telling stories about the magnificent benefits of simple acts of kindness.*

2.  *Write one story from your list in (4) describing FROM/TO transformations in your life.*

3.  *Write stories when someone was a hero to you. Tell us a story when you were a hero to someone else or when you acted heroically.*

# CHAPTER 4

# Apprenticing Generations of Master Builders

*He said, "come to the edge of the cliff."*
*They said, "we are afraid."*
*He said, "come to the edge of the cliff."*
*They said, "we are afraid."*
*They came.*
*He pushed.*
*They flew.*

—*Guillaume Appollinanine*

Cathedral building spanned multiple generations because families were purposeful in apprenticing their children. The system of apprenticeship was first developed in the Middle Ages. The master architect chose his master builders – master quarryman, master stonecutter, master sculptor, master mortar maker, master mason, master carpenter, master blacksmith, master glass maker. Each ran his own workshop with assistants and apprentices. A master craftsman was entitled to employ young people, typically ten to fifteen years old, as an inexpensive form of labor in exchange for food, lodging, and training in a craft that was to become their lifelong profession. Apprenticing was a learning experience not from classrooms, but from hands-on practice in workshops and worksites. The best way to learn about blacksmithing is from a master blacksmith making the tools for the masons. Practical application shaped skill proficiency. It was at times fun, exhausting, boring, and thrilling. When the apprenticeship ended usually in seven years, the apprentice was considered a journeyman and travelled seeking their profession's work. Apprentices aspired to be master craftsmen themselves.

The relationship between master and apprentice was often as close as that between parent and child. Apprentices lived in their master's house or shop; they usually ate with the master's family, often wore clothes provided by the master, and were subject to the master's house rules and discipline. The relationship was intimate and apprentices often formed close emotional bonds with the master's family including marrying daughters. Apprentices were even remembered in their master's will!

Apprenticing prepares your family. Under the watchful eye of master craftsmen, clumsy hands become careful. Impatience is overcome with a plan. A hole in the ground becomes a foundation. Pieces of wood become a curvilinear buttress. Rocks expertly measured and placed become a column. A formless shape becomes a vaulted ceiling. Limestone by itself isn't all that useful. It's just rock. But through the keen apportioning of quarryman, the rock is chiseled – part artistry, skill, diligence, experience – into a stone. Sand by itself isn't all that useful until it is skillfully transformed into molten glass, mixed with miniscule metals powders, and intricately placed into the lattice of lead pieces to form stained glass motifs.

Apprenticing is a path of self-discovery that prepares your family to be life-ready. Are your apprentices not just skilled, but ready for life? Not only did master builders impart their apprentices with the skills to become great carpenters, masons, stonecutters, and glass blowers, but they also fostered confidence. They replaced timidity with sureness. They supplanted clumsiness with poise and determination. They prepared them to be more than skilled masons. Men teach boys to become gentlemen. Women teach girls to become ladies. Manhood and womanhood isn't something that just happens to boys and girls as they anatomically grow. Without apprenticing they will crash through moral guardrails. Without apprenticing they may heap a mountain of debt. They will follow the clearest, most consistent voice. Do you rise above the drone of friends and culture? They need to be more than taught; you need to demonstrate. Without a role model, boys do not naturally become gentlemen. Master architects are responsible for managing the transition to adulthood.

Do they know themselves and have a vision for their life?

Are they seeking their passion?

Are they developing their gifts?

Do they value and esteem people?

Are they gritty, resilient and persevering under trying circumstances?

Are they pursuing excellence in whatever they do?

Are they learning continuously and growing?

Are they caring, compassionate, gentle, altruistic, generous?

Are they self-disciplined and responsible?

Are they gentlemen who honor women?

Are they living their faith and nurturing their beliefs?

*Dear Nicholas,*

*It was pelting rain, wind to our faces and very cold. We could hardly see in front of us, let alone navigate the miles of open lakes to reach portages to hop skip lakes to reach our ultimate destination – the Canadian border. You carried our gear, our food, our supplies – nearly as much as you weighed – across hilltop portages. The wind was so strong that missing a stroke pushed us backwards. But you did it without complaining and with a steadfast, strong-willed spirit that astonished me. When the treacherous weather deflated my ideal expectations for this trip with you – we never reached the border - you reframed it for me when you said, "Dad, I'm just so happy to be here with you." And as we opened our hearts to each other over fires and meals, the knot between us tightened. That unmarked island you navigated with a simple map and compass was more than a refuge, it was a turning point for us. On that canoe trip, I learned how strong and resilient you are. You taught me the journey matters more than the destination. Love, Dad*

*Life-ready instills the Principle of the Path.* Most of us don't know where we are going because we are too busy to think about it. Do they understand that the path they choose leads to a destination? Do they understand that their choices are powerful, but could make them utterly powerless? We need to encourage them to pre-determine the story they want to tell. We need to consistently reinforce the fresh relevancy of path choices throughout a lifetime, not just when they are adolescents. Dating, engagement, newlyweds, parenting, first jobs, layoffs, direct reports, debt, prodigal children, health crisis, caregiving – life doesn't happen in one exam. Anticipate and prepare them for the choices they will encounter. Consider the transitions not as fleeting and incongruent headlines, but more like harmonious life chapters with common themes centered on their purpose and vision.

> "We make a living by what we get, but we make a life by what we give." — Winston Churchill

One story. I selfishly wasted my twenties. Nothing seemed interesting to me, nothing inspired me outside work, so I spent all my time working or blowing time playing videogames and watching television. I was successful at work – moving up the ladder, getting kudos from my bosses and less so from my jealous peers – but there was still something missing, an emptiness that I couldn't put my finger on . . .

A better story. I decided early that I wanted balance in my life. I wanted to work hard, learn, and grow as a professional, but I also wanted to do something important outside work. I tried different things – being a Big Brother to foster kids, tutoring kids struggling in school – and I landed on something I was deeply passionate about so I . . .

One story. I became so enthralled with winning at work and amassing wealth and power that I somehow forgot that I had a family. Because my wife seemed to handle everything without me, I neglected to give her any encouragement, gratitude, or affection. She seemed to be okay with me being so devoted to work and we certainly enjoined spending money, but I wasn't listening to her begging for me to slow down and spend time with her. I became more devoted to my colleagues at work then her. We eventually drifted so far apart; we barely knew each other and then....

A better story. I decided early that if I was going to cheat with my limited time being pulled at work and home, I would cheat work over family. I love my work, enjoy it every day, but my family brings out the best in me. I'm irreplaceable at home. Instead of rushing through homework like it was a race or hurrying through bedtime routines, I savored the tiny moments of apprenticing the next generation of cathedral builders in our family.

*Rya, Tali, and David,*

*I am shaped today by the generations before me. My great paternal grandfather, Louis Harris came to the United States with nothing and starting selling brooms door-to-door. Through persistence and hard work, he sold enough brooms to purchase a cart. Then he started selling other household cleaning items, still door-to-door. Eventually he sold enough brooms to open a store. That store became the largest department store in Montclair, NJ. Today you can go to Montclair and see a plaque with his name in that location and a pizza restaurant named after him called Louis'. From this story, which my father told me on a regular basis, I learned that if you work hard and take advantage of opportunities, you can be successful. With love, Mom*

## 4.1 Quarry Questions

1. *Make a list of story starters that illuminate the path choices your family will encounter over their life at home and work, in relationships, and regarding finances, health, and spirituality. Highlight the vastly dissimilar destinations from different path choices.*

## 4.1 Legacy Letters

1. *Choose a few of the story starters depicting the path choices you made; in hindsight portray the dreadful and jubilant consequences.*

2. *Write a story about something someone said or did that profoundly impacted the direction of your life.*

*Apprenticing requires mastery.* Apprenticing others to build your family cathedral is a calling. Master builders didn't just encourage apprentices to try their best; they pursued excellence. They were hard without being harsh; they were exacting without expecting immediate perfectionism; they were hands-on teachers without sheltering. At its core, legacy apprenticing is about imprinting your life skills, know-how, and values so that naiveté is replaced with wisdom, immaturity withers and responsibility ripens. Apprenticing means you don't protect them from or hide them from or do for them because . . . Rather you allow them to embrace small failures because it matures them. Apprenticing doesn't mean you take away the hurt and pain, but you empathetically share stories about how to handle it, overcome it, rebound from it. Ordinary boys become men through personal hardship. Girls become women when they overcome trials. Apprenticing primes them to be the next generation of master builders, but it is something they must earn, something they must achieve, something with which they will necessarily struggle. They need to hear from you that they have to fail or struggle or blunder to learn. Apprenticing forms deep roots and then gives wings for apprentices to journey on their own.

*Dear Leah, Carly, and Lucy,*

*Growing up is hard work. There is so much that changes in your first eighteen years. You go from not being able to walk or eat by yourselves to being fully physically independent. The physical changes are the most noticeable, but are also the easiest. You are going to get bigger and stronger no matter what you do – you are going to grow. Growing up emotionally is what takes the most work. It is hard and at times you will want to revert back to childlike ways – times when it was okay to be selfish like when you were two years old. However, it is our growth emotionally that really transforms us into the adults that we will be. And you will be an adult much longer than you are a child.*

*When I was in fourth grade there was a field day at my school – it was called Up, Up, and Away Day. We had never had one before and to my recollection we never had one again. So, it was truly a once-in-a lifetime experience in my elementary school.*

*The field day was after school hours and because your grandmother worked, I was a little late arriving. Once I got there, I sought out my friends. I spotted them across the track and started walking towards them. They spotted me and turned to walk in the other direction. I was hurt, confused and sad. Why were they walking away? None of them would talk to me. When it came time to do the Tug of War, they replaced me on the team with another girl that we barely knew. I was devastated.*

*I have no idea why they treated me that way on that day. The significance of watching my friends walk away from me for reasons I did not understand stuck with me though. I learned a significant lesson that day. I never wanted to make anyone feel the way that I felt that day. You might say they helped me grow up emotionally. I would have rather learned that lesson any other way than having my feelings hurt, but nevertheless, I learned the lesson.*

*Now, you may assume that day was the end of my friendship with those girls. However, our friendship soon returned and we were playing at recess and having sleepovers. You see, I believe they were learning an emotional lesson that day too. They learned that they didn't like to make someone cry. They didn't like to see someone be by themselves with no one to play with. I don't remember anything significant that returned our friendships to normal in fourth grade, but they did. And this may surprise you, but all of them are still my friends today.*

*As you grow up, remember that all of your friends are growing up too. You all will do things to hurt each other or be selfish at times, but you will learn from those times. You will do selfish acts less and less, and one day you will find that you are an adult who has grown not just in physical size, but in your emotional heart as well. I love you. Love, Mommy*

Legacy building insists on intricate details – the quality and placement of every stone, the temperature of the molten sand for the stained glass, the moisture content in the mortar. Every detail matters. When master carpenters apprenticed, they were methodical and intentional about the skills of carpentry – flush edges, exacting corner cuts, double pole scaffold, floor framing stability under load. Master builders didn't just ensure their mentees followed their process, but they simultaneously explained "why." *"Why do we need to . . . Why does it work that way . . . Why can't we just . . . "* Master builders anticipated that their imaginative learners wouldn't blindly follow their rules; they satisfied their natural curiosity to be original. They taught the principles of their craft and emboldened their originality. One master builder and his team of apprentices discovered the flying buttress, devised the vaulted ceiling, designed the first stained glass template.

*Dear Jordan,*

*One day in the first couple of years of school you asked me if you could give a friend something special because they had given you a treat. Now I can't remember exactly what it was (probably a sparkly eraser or fluffy pencil or some such given your penchant at the time for all things "special"). You were definite that it needed to be something big (and no doubt super, super sparkly).*

*You were always very generous giving things to people and you felt so good doing it, but I had to explain that sometimes by doing even the most generous thing you can make a person feel bad. Feel like they have to do the same thing, even when they couldn't or weren't able to. Being generous is more than giving things. We are very lucky and privileged to live the way we do, but what we have doesn't count. It's who we are, how we treat others and the people we hold close to us that is most important.*

*I know that at times I'm not the best role model. We didn't have much when we were growing up and Gramps struggled with the pressures of everyday life. So now that I'm a mum I take great delight in being able to give you a life that I did not have. But we have to remember that what you have is more than the things you have around you. It's the fact that you and I can sit down and play a fast and furious game of cards or can companionably sit side by side (shhhh don't tell Dada as he would prefer you sat in the back) driving somewhere. The fact that we can laugh and laugh over role playing 'wind in our hair like puppy dogs' or hugging and simply saying "night night, I love you" at the end of a busy day. That's what really counts, and by doing what we do each day, you remind me of that and hopefully I can help remind you . . . so that you stop saying "If ever there was a flood I'd have to save all my clothes!" Love, Mama*

Apprenticing develops master builders too. You cannot apprentice what you haven't mastered. They will follow your example and mimic what they see you doing. Are you role modelling what you teach? We all do better when someone is watching. We stop expressing trite expressions like "never tell a lie" and start living up to them. As a young father of my three-year-old, I'll never forget when he first told me I lied to him. After asking relentlessly about going to the park later in the day on a Saturday, I told him "maybe" or "we'll try to get there." Kids don't understand "maybe" and they certainly don't understand "trying" to go somewhere – you just go somewhere or you don't. It was nearly bedtime and he asked when we were going to the park. Exhausted and tired, I told him, "It's dark and too late; not today." Crying, he told me that I lied to him. I unknowingly broke a tacit promise. As innocent as this was, it was a teachable moment for me as a dad and I started being clearer with my kids.

"Contrary to popular misguided cultural stereotypes and frequent parental misperceptions, the evidence clearly shows that the single most important social influence on the religious and spiritual lives of adolescents is their parents . . . Parents are the most important determinant of their children's spiritual life – or lack thereof." — Smith and Denton, Soul Searching

How would your kids introduce you? What if how you were introduced became something you strived for? I sat in an elementary school classroom and the teacher surprised the parents with some guessing games. Dads had to correctly guess their son or daughter's answer from the class' multiple choice responses. The answers were revealing.

*What's your favorite thing to do with your Dad?* "Wrestle with my dad and brothers in the basement." "Play video games while my mom works." "Nothing."

*What's a super hero quality you have?* "I'm fast as lightning – faster than my dad." "My big mouth."

*What does your Dad tell you all the time?* "How much he loves me." "Be quiet."

When we are mindful of legacy building suddenly every detail matters – how we spend our time, our emotional temperament at home, weekend behavior that cannot be divorced from weekday behavior. She notices the little things. He absorbs your mannerisms and motives. You need to pre-decide what stories you want them to tell about being mentored by you. Legacy building causes us to live more consistently in our marriage, our work, our parenting, our finances, our faith. It is so easy to live inconsistently because circumstances and occasions can push us on the margin to say or do something "out of character." Often no one holds us accountable for our contradictions. They *seem* to slip by family members, but they really don't. Consider the apprenticing contradictions illuminated in an article published by Alison Cooper in *The Washington Post*:

*. . . a dad and his two sons, roughly 8 and 10, piled into the car next to mine, and in so doing one of the boys carelessly flung his door open so far that it scraped the side of my car . . . I was appalled to see the dad backing out of his parking spot, apparently with no intention of stopping. I aborted my call and leaped out of my car, screaming at the driver. At this point he stopped, got out of his car and began [yelling]: It's a ding! This is a parking lot, what do you expect! What's the big deal?! Get some touch-up paint! . . . I let him go, feeling slightly . . . sick about the lesson he had just taught his boys:*

1.  *When you damage someone else's car, try to get away without having to face the owner of the car, and*

2.  *If this fails, come out swinging aggressively, minimize the damage, and assert that parking-lot dings are a fact of life . . .*

*The next day my seven-year-old daughter pointed out to me fresh and severe damage to the bumper. It was badly crunched. We were home in our driveway, but the damage could have occurred anytime during the previous 24 hours while we were out and about on errands. There was no note on the windshield. I sadly accepted that I'd never know who did this to my car . . .*

*The next day, a husband and wife came to my home to explain what happened. The wife, in halting English, explained that their son had panicked after hitting the car and rushed to them . . . They notified their insurance company and then went looking for the damaged car . . . They provided their insurance information and apologized profusely. These parents taught their teenage son:*

1.  *Take responsibility for your actions, even if you can get away with not doing so, even if it's not convenient or easy, and even though your insurance rates are certain to increase with this acknowledgement, and*

2.  *Don't make excuses, don't lie, be forthcoming and apologize."*

Purposeful legacy writing shoves inconsistency aside. When we contemplate the stories we want to leave behind to our families, we become so much more aware of our patchy behavior. Mindful legacy building causes us to become intolerant of duplicity. We have an immense capacity to deceive ourselves and make convenient exceptions. But when you feel answerable to your legacy, everything matters – the seen and the unseen – because generations will follow you. Master builders are always on stage. Are our behaviors aligned with our words and our words aligned with our values and vision? Not just during sit-at-the-kitchen-table discussions when someone did something wrong. Do we consistently pass our own Kindergarten Test – the things we tell our kids at the earliest ages?

> *Share.* Who eats the last piece of pie, the last cookie, the first piece of cake? How do you spend your weekend time? When have you been exceedingly generous?

> *Be thankful for what you have.* Your kids ever see you envious – what *they* drive, what *they* wear, where *they* live, how *they* look?

> *Never lie.* Ever have your kids catch you stretching the truth? No shades of gray – just the black and white of it.

> *Tattletaling isn't nice.* Your kids ever see you gossip? Backbite? Say something sassy about someone else? Try to hurt someone back for hurting you?

> *Be brave.* Ever feel or act like a chicken?

> *Always apologize for doing something wrong?* Ever hold back a few hours or days to forgive so someone owes you? Are your apologies sincere or half-hearted?

> *Don't waste.* Do you always wear the clothes or shoes you bought? Ever blow an entire Sunday recovering from Saturday night?

*Wait your turn.* Ever impatient driving, waiting in line, with slow servers?

*Don't be a sore loser.* Are you fun to play games with or only when you are winning?

*Be respectful of those in authority.* What impression do your kids have about your boss despite never meeting him/her? How do you talk to your mom or dad?

*Help others even when you don't get anything in return.* Do you help only with strings attached?

*Don't make fun of others' differences.* Ever talk about someone's haircut, their weight or their age?

*Do to others as you want them to do to you.* Do you treat everyone with honor and respect regardless of their position or stature?

*Dear Jonathan, Nicholas and Rachel*

*I was a newly appointed leader of a small business unit– very green and only a few years out of MBA school. My counterpart in the business was a sharp, middle-aged retired Air Force captain, Pete. Almost immediately he struck a rivalry. Nothing tense, but teasing. In fact, Pete's persona at work was that of a "commander." A few years into my role, Pete had stroke. I took over his responsibilities for several months while he rehabilitated. When Pete came back to work, it was clear he wasn't 100%. But the respect, patience and effort that our boss and his team provided him astounded me. Despite falling behind in our financial objectives, the team pulled together and rallied around Pete to deliver his results. I'll never forget a quarterly financial review with our CEO and*

*CFO. Pete struggled with his logic, but with slurred words he proudly reviewed his outstanding results . . . with the confidence he always had. Our boss and executives patiently allowed him to review his material despite repeating items several times. They honored someone who had dedicated many years to Kimberly-Clark, not by pandering to him or being dismissive because of his inadequacies, but dignifying his dedication. I hope you choose to work for a company that reflects your personal values especially those companies that are courageous enough in those defining moments to put people first. It makes it easy to get up every day and go to work. Love, Dad*

Get into the habit of having your kids look over your shoulder. Think about them sitting alongside you in meetings before you pound your chest. Think about them sitting at the coffee shop with gossiping friends. Think about them in the company of your friends telling crude jokes. Someday your family will look back on their life and recall the simple lessons from their master builder not based on what you said, but the example you showed them.

*Dear Jonathan, Nicholas and Rachel,*

*Build a reputation for developing others at work. Build a reputation for being a leader who serves others and brings out the best in them…and yes, even surpass you. It might seem wimpy. It might seem archaic. It might seem professionally reckless. You might not get the recognition that you deserve. But your significance, your legacy isn't built on exceeding sales or nailing timelines. Sure, these are important. But they aren't lasting. Develop a reputation for developing the potential in others. You may never get a promotion for it, but you'll receive something far more significant – the satisfaction of helping someone flourish.*

*"Hi Bruce! I wanted to give you some feedback that I heard a couple of days ago. I was taking a communications course with Stephanie the other day and a big part of the course was focused on listening. She was talking about how she wants to be like people she knows who really seem like they listen AND actually care when you are talking (among other things, but that was the gist) – and when she said that you automatically popped into my mind! So I asked her who she has interacted with here that does that and she said, "The only person I can really think of is Bruce Williamson." I said , "That's exactly who popped into my head!" You've had a huge impact on lots of people! Take care, and I hope things are going well for you!"*

*You'll receive plenty of accolades over the years, but I tell you with confidence that nothing makes you hold your head higher than mentoring and growing others. Let that be your mark on the world. Love, Dad*

## 4.2 Quarry Questions

1. *When are your behaviors and words most consistent with your vision? Most inconsistent or patchy? Do you pass your own the Kindergarten Test?*

2. *Ask your kids what three words describe you.*

3. *Ask your kids how they would introduce you. How do you want to be introduced by your children?*

4. *What "Promise me . . ." statements do you want your apprentices to follow like True North?*

*4.2 Legacy Letters*

1.  *Write letters explaining longings you have for your apprentices.*

2.  *Write stories about when they have reflected your apprenticing instruction and how proud it made you feel.*

*Entrust others to apprentice.* Master craftsmen from distinctive professions would work alongside each other, integrating their skills for a shared common vision for their cathedral. Quarrymen would lift stones from the quarry then they would be cut, chiseled, hammered by the stonecutter to match the template provided by the master mason. Many of the skilled workers relied on other trades to keep them at work. A master blacksmith made all the metal tools for masons, while skilled carpenters made the wooden handles for these tools. Carpenters made the hoists, scaffolding, and platforms for quarrymen. Clever master craftsmen would have their apprentices learn other skills – stonecutter apprentices would spend time in the carpenter workshop and carpenter apprentices would spend time on the construction site with the master stonecutter.

---

"There is no enduring culture in which parents attempt this task [transitioning to adulthood] alone."
— Dr. Leonard Sax, Boys Adrift

---

Many of us have had strong influences from people other than our parents in our lives. It could have been a coach, an aunt or uncle, a close family friend, or even a boss. When others apprentice, they have the unique ability to speak congruent wisdom but from a different context. When parents speak about the importance of choosing the right friends, our children may seem dismissive because it's expected. Yet when an uncle talks about his wayward years in high school choosing improper friends, the dramatic wrong turns leading to a vivid "night in jail" story, somehow it penetrates, it sticks. Attention to parental messaging waxes and wanes over time. It's a natural byproduct of children establishing their own independence and emerging self-leadership. It's not that the parental message isn't relevant or it's not compelling enough. It's not even something kinked in your relationships. Our kids naturally appeal life coaching from others. Dr. Leonard Sax in <u>Boys Adrift</u> states, "Find a community that can give your son healthy and life affirming examples of what it means to be a man...without a community they will look elsewhere for role models . . . Shortly after a Navajo girl experiences her first menstrual period, she is sequestered in the hut of her grandmother for four consecutive days. During those four days, all of her adult female relatives call on her. She engages in a series of rituals illustrating her new status as a woman in her community." Once my son was listening to a particularly compelling story about some poor teen choices made by an adult friend of our family. My son was captivated. There was nothing novel about the message on teen drinking, but the messenger was different. My son said something revealing: "I expected you to say that, Dad, but not Mr. Joe." We need the furtherance of others to apprentice our family. We can't build a cathedral on our own. Who else should be apprenticing your family? Who else can be an indistinguishable voice to your growing boys faced with peer pressure to drinking beer and collect women like trophies? Who shares your beliefs but can instruct in another way?

*Victoria, Jacob Thomas, Matthew, Mark William, Lucas, and Zachary,*

*When I was in junior high school, my uncle Jack Knapp visited us from Boston. One day he decided to treat many of the cousins to a day at our amusement park Valley Fair. My uncle was keen at orchestrating breakthroughs, to get you to do things that you never thought you could do. With his coaxing I had swam across the length of a pool, which seemed beyond*

*my capabilities and jump off of a big dive board. It is a pow-*
*erful thing to overcome your fears and be more of who you*
*are created to be. So, looking back, I should not be surprised*
*at my uncle's insistence to ride the corkscrew triple-loop roller*
*coaster. However, this time I dug my heels in hard and he kept*
*pushing me to the point where things got emotional, due to*
*our mutual stubbornness. It seemed that the stalemate would*
*never end, when finally I either mustered up the courage to go*
*or gave into the social pressure. Well, you can imagine how I*
*felt when I was strapped in and the roller coaster was climbing*
*the hill; I was beyond the point of no return and felt I had*
*made a big mistake with each click of the roller coaster is it*
*ascended to the crest. What was surprising is how fun it was*
*and how much I enjoyed the ride. I wanted to go again and*
*again. It is not wise to take foolish risks in life, but sometimes*
*you have to get out of your comfort zone or else miss out on the*
*joys that life has to offer. Love, Daddy*

---

"Our memory competes with the onslaught of information. We should find a place to preserve them, and the safest place is not our own vessel because we will inevitably lose it or break it. We tend to be less careful with the things we give ourselves, but when we receive gifts, we treat them with nurturing care. The way to preserve our memories is to give them as gifts to others." — Richard Louv, Web of Life

---

Our life stories are inherently limited. You can only apprentice from what you have experienced. If you want your kids to understand the consequences and aftermath, the advantages and adulation of certain experiences, you may not be in a position to write with Perspective or a Pure Heart. Identify people who have a sphere of influence to apprentice your family. Identify the blacksmiths, the glass blowers, the masons, the architects to bring their diverse experiences to create guardrails for your teens or inspire your son in his fathering or encourage your granddaughter in her self-image search. If you haven't experienced the tragedy of divorce, find a master carpenter who has. If you haven't experienced the tragedy of abandonment, find a master blacksmith who has. If you don't know how to handle a difficult boss or job loss, find a master mason who does. Ask them to write a letter and share their life lessons. Bring your story stones to others' cathedrals. Write letters to your nieces and nephews, children of family friends, students, players. Apprenticing others may be the most important thing that you do, and it certainly allows you to carve your initials in legacy stones that will outlive you.

Insecure parents worry that their stories may be inferior to others, that they will lose influence. The outcome we desire as master builders is a well-apprenticed son, daughter, grandson, or granddaughter. The goal isn't to have the most enthralling stories, but to penetrate through the clutter of culture and instill lifelong wisdom that can be conjured on-demand during life's toughest decisions, choices and trials. Cathedrals are built with togetherness. To create a community apprenticing approach to building your family legacy, we need to ask for others to bring their teachable story stones and we need to spontaneously provide story stones to others' cathedrals.

*Learn from other cathedral builders.* The master architect gained his knowledge of architecture and engineering by visiting and working on numerous cathedrals across Europe. He was a student of others' cathedrals across his travels, inspired by their methods, encouraged by their new techniques. Allow others' stories to provide a new vantage to the life lessons you want inculcated in your family. Observe how other master builders apprentice. Develop a cadence of connection with other cathedral builders on a regular basis.

*4.3 Quarry Questions*

1. *Who can give your son or daughter healthy and life-affirming examples of what it means to be a man or woman, the paths to avoid and those to follow?*

2. *Who are other cathedral builders you can learn from?*

*4.3 Legacy Lessons*

1. *What lessons do you want taught to your family, but with which you have no experience? Who can write these stories?*

2. *Write stories to those outside your family for whom you have influence. Write the stories they will need today and in the future to be master builders themselves.*

*Apprentice up.* Master craftsman are skilled and experienced but they desire encouragement and reassurance too. Apprentices should not assume that their instructors are tirelessly aplomb and effortlessly ebullient. Not in the form of cheering or boasting or praising, but from feedback. Mentoring can be incredibly lonely and full of doubt. *Is my mentoring working? Are they listening? Am I getting through? Are they are growing under my headship?* Apprentices, bring story stones to the cathedral by writing letters to your mentoring master craftsman. Shine a light on how their apprenticing mattered. Wrap your arms around their shoulder, sit beside them, hold their hand and tell them in your own words the difference they made. Let them hear it from you. In your words. With your affection. With tears on the paper. With a big grin. With springy hope in your heart. In a way that only you can communicate to your mom and dad or grandparents. Don't assume that they know – the tragedy of the ungiven gift of gratitude stings. There are few things more treasured to sacrificing parents than to hear words of affirmation from their children. There are few things more cherished to devoted grandparents, aunts, uncles, adult mentors than to read a letter of gratitude recounting influence in the life of someone they have poured countless hours caring for, worrying about, hoping for, praying for, cheering for, believing in, loving boundlessly.

*Dear Mama and Papa,*

*Courage. Faith. Family. Constancy. Love. Hard Work. Adventure. These are what I think of when think of you. You have a history of doing wildly brave things. You were married in Cuba and almost immediately made a leap of faith in coming to the United States, flying into Miami and riding on a bus to NYC while speaking next to no English, and never knowing that political events would cause a permanent separation in your family that you bore with such grace and courage. You both wanted to be successful in America and worked so hard to achieve that. Papa – you created such a unique legacy in helping to make Bibles as part of your job. Mama – though, legally blind, you used your immense sewing talents to become a prominent seamstress at Simplicity, even sowing items for Fashion Week. You created a home where I always felt loved and special, a place where Steve and I could spend hours playing with amazing train sets, begging Papa to "fix us up," eating delicious food, and looking through sewing patterns of the latest fashions.*

*When my dad took his own leap of faith and made a wildly brave career change and move to Florida, you once again showed courage and left your current life behind, determined to make a new life in Florida just to be near your only child, son-in-law, and grandchildren. My father, left parentless by the time he was 30, was adopted by you in every way that matters. You showed him unconditional love and supported his choices to better the life of his family. While he went back to school and my mom became a working parent for the first time in our lives, you were there. You made sure we were taken care of and happy.*

*Your faith constantly moves me. "Trust in the Lord." You say it so much that the phrase is forever intertwined with my memories of you. Because of you, I have had the courage and sense of adventure to take chances, trusting God completely with the outcome. Thank you for your love, your legacy, and for your example. Love, Stephanie ("la chicatica de la casa")*

Just as children thrive when they are noticed by parents, concomitantly master builders find satisfaction knowing their apprenticing matters. Enable mentors to see their difference in your life. Express your gratitude. Assure them that their instruction has stuck with you. Commit to them that you will finish the great unfinished work of building a cathedral of family legacy.

### 4.4 Quarry Questions

1. *How would you introduce your father? What labels do you have for him – my protector, my hero, my life coach, my wise sounding board? How would you introduce your mother? What labels do you have for her – my cheerleader, my best friend, my rock?*

2. *Do your parents know how much it meant when they stood up for you? When they cheered you on? When they had your back? When they didn't sway even when you broke their heart?*

### 4.4 Legacy Lessons

1. *Write story stones to your parents, grandparents, brothers, sisters, aunts, uncles, friends, coaches. Have them see the difference they made in your life. Tell them why their lesson/instruction mattered then and still now. Point out which stones in your cathedral are cut from them.*

2. *Tell us a story about . . .*

*When did your mom/dad help you believe in yourself?*

*When did your mom/dad make your heart swell with love?*

*When did your mom/dad make you smile on the inside – full of worthiness and satisfaction?*

*When you were glad that your mom/dad was tough on you?*

*When did they make you proud?*

*When were they your hero?*

*When did you secretly use their advice and were so grateful you did?*

Apprenticing bears fruit. Apprenticing gives them the confidence to jump not because you are the helicopter parent, but because they know your parachute works. Do they know you love them wholly, unconditionally, completely? What happens when mentors believe in apprentices in unexpected ways that they never realized? They pick up the tools and continue building your family cathedral. They aren't just leaving a legacy, but leading one.

In our hyper-scheduled, busy lives we feel toxically depleted. We feel too empty to give; we may even feel resentment. We prioritize the tangible things – projects, appointments – over the intangibles – family time, relationship time, spiritual time. Paradoxically, the antidote for the bitter busyness in our lives isn't getting more done; its connection – with others and your faith. We can easily settle into the counterfeit life of "fitting in." We can easily get swept into the self-propaganda of being "needed at work." We are immune to the repetitiveness and we say, "I don't have time. I'm too busy." What if there's a bigger picture and you are missing out? Pay-it-forward; give back because someone gave to you.

Every stonecutter had a distinguishing mark which he engraved on every stone so the quality of his work could be evaluated in order to be paid. A father handed his mark down to his son, but the son would add a variation of his own. Stone marks became the personal pride of families, overt and inescapable signatures of their collective esteem for generations. What are the distinguishing marks in stone of your family? Have you told them?

In 2013, the US Department of Health and Human Services found that that the average cost of raising a child was over $4000 per year excluding college. What do you get for that vast sum of money? What do you get for that investment? No-strings-attached love. To be called "Mom" or "Dad." To be a hero. A glimpse of God every day. To shepherd their growth from apprentices to master builders of your family legacy.

Pre-define your legacy. What vision do you have for your family that's too big to fit neatly inside your head, but can only fit in your heart? What stories do you want your family to tell over and over again? What lessons took you a lifetime to learn, but you don't want them to take a lifetime to learn? What is the impression your life makes? What is your imprint on others? Your answer matters to the generations behind you that carry your name, that call you Mom or Dad, Grandmom or Grandpop, or Aunt or Uncle. Today, start the lifelong journey of apprenticing generations of your family to build the great unfinished work of your family legacy. Stone by stone. Enduring family stories marked in stone.

Made in the USA
Lexington, KY
18 December 2014